AF657565

MADHYA PRADESH

Unhurried Unspoilt Undiscovered

MADHYA PRADESH

Unhurried Unspoilt Undiscovered

Probir Sen

The heart of Incredible India
Madhya Pradesh Tourism

wisdom tree

First published in 2010 by
Wisdom Tree
4779/23
Ansari Road
Darya Ganj
New Delhi - 110002
Phone: 91 - 11 - 23247966/ 67/ 68
wisdomtreebooks@gmail.com

The project has been supported by Madhya Pradesh State Tourism Development Corporation Limited.

Printed in India.

Text © Probir Sen
Photographs © Madhya Pradesh Tourism; Madhyam (p. 18, 32, 34, 66, 72, 75, 79, 80); Bhalu Mondhe (p. 64-65); Shobit Arya (p. 33); Hari Mahidhar/Dinodia Images (p. 82).

All rights reserved. No part of this publication may be reproduced, or transmitted in any form or by any means, without the prior permission of the author and the publisher.

ISBN 978-81-8328-151-5

Design: tiffinbox

Front cover: *Spectacular reflections from the past—Jahaz Mahal, Mandu.*
Back cover: *The verdant glory of Pachmarhi.*

CONTENTS

ॐ
नर्मदे हर

PREFACE

Why, it may well be asked, should there be yet another volume on places of tourist attractions in Madhya Pradesh when, in fact a number of excellent guide books on these places exist, published by the Archaeological Survey of India and the M.P. State Tourism Development Corporation.

The only explanation I can offer for this attempt is that it is not a guide book. These essays are intended to provide an introduction to the places covered, something that will hopefully persuade tourists to visit, stay, and imbibe more about these places by reading and interacting with the people living there.

Unlike many other states in India Madhya Pradesh does not evoke one single image. This is partly because it does not possess typical attractions such as the mountains or the sea, and partly because its immensity and the astonishing variety of what it does have to offer do not permit its confinement to a stereotype.

LEFT

Early morning view of Shri Omkar Mandhata Temple, Omkareshwar, on the banks of River Narmada.

Geographically, Madhya Pradesh is located in the heart of India. It is also true that India's ancient and eternal spirit resides here. Spending time in the state is, therefore, not just seeing places, but experiencing the essence of India – the pristine magic of its forests, the restrained magnificence of its monuments, the exuberance of crowds in festivals, and the great peace the solitude and silence bring.

Madhya Pradesh is the second largest state in the country, sprawling over 3,08,000 square kilometres. It has a very large proportion of India's forests and hence numerous natural parks and sanctuaries, including Kanha and Bandhavgarh, which are amongst the finest in the country. Apart from forests, there is also the vast plateau, the hill ranges of the Vindhyas and Satpuras and the great rivers flowing across it: the Narmada, Tapti, Chambal, Sone, Betwa and Ken. Its climate is by and large moderate, and its people warm and gentle, with a tolerance that has enabled all the major faiths to exist and flourish – Hinduism, Islam, Jainism and Buddhism. Vast tracts of the state are also enriched by the unique and precious culture of its tribes.

Close to Nature, sometimes surrounded by it, and often competing with it in magnificence, are the monuments of Madhya Pradesh. Being located in the centre of India, all trade routes across the country, from north to south, had to pass through Madhya Pradesh. The resultant commerce, together with the wealth of its soil and the rivers, brought great prosperity to the area. While it had contact with all parts of India, it was fortunately just south of the region that suffered constant invasions. This rare combination of wealth and absence of depredations has left the state with over one thousand monuments and many more antiquities, in an almost perfect state of preservation, ranging in time from the prehistoric to the modern.

Not being fortunate enough to have been born or brought up in Madhya Pradesh, I nevertheless have had the excitement of having lived and worked in the state for over a decade. I was, and remain, totally captivated by its attractions; the state for me being an enormous retreat from the tumult and turmoil of living in the national capital, never failing to provide solace, inspiration and invigoration. Madhya Pradesh remains for me unhurried, unspoilt, and to a great extent, undiscovered. It is hoped that these essays would serve as an hors d'oeuvre to what I am sure would be a continuous and rewarding experience for any visitor to the state.

I have, for factual material, drawn from the fine guidebooks of the Archaeological Survey of India and the M.P. State Tourism Development Corporation Eicher guide on Madhya Pradesh, something which I would like to gratefully acknowledge.

I would also like to express my gratitude to Shri B. M. Pande the distinguished archaeologist, who was with the Archaeological Survey of India, for having spared the time to go through my text; to Ashok and Rahul Noronha and Dr Faiqa Saulat

Map not to scale.
For representational purposes only.

Khan, eminent and knowledgeable citizens of Bhopal who pointed out factual errors after going through my pieces; to my colleagues Shri Sudesh Gupta and Shri S.C. Kumar who assisted me in the task of preparing the manuscript, without which it would have never emerged; and finally, and most importantly, to Shri Shobit Arya and his colleagues of Wisdom Tree publication, and Shri Ashwini Lohani, Managing Director of the M.P. State Tourism Development Corporation, who have given me the opportunity to write this book.

I would like to end by stating that it was for me a great pleasure to mentally revisit these places that I cherish in Madhya Pradesh, even though time did not permit me the joy of going to them physically; however this is something I will continue to do for the rest of my life.

GWALIOR - SHIVPURI - ORCHHA

Gwalior | All those who travel on the *Dakshinapatha*, the principal north-south trade route that connected the wealthy kingdoms of the north to the sea ports on the western coast have to pass through Gwalior, for it is the gateway to Madhya Desh – India's heartland. The drive is like the passage through any of our overgrown towns – a tortuous struggle through crowds, chaos, narrow encroached-upon streets, smoke, dust, more crowds, and one longs only to leave it all behind, till one looks up. There, dominating and protecting the city, but well above it, is the fort astride a large hill – massive, masculine, brooding.

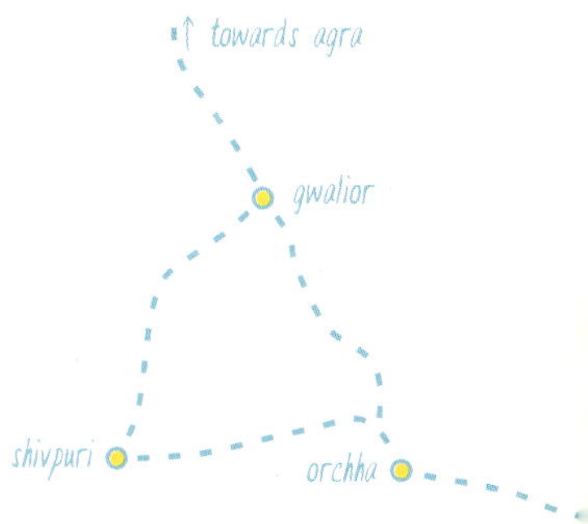

LEFT

The imposing exterior of the Man Mandir Palace, Gwalior Fort.

ABOVE

Decorative detail on the wall of Man Mandir Palace, Gwalior Fort.

And if one pauses to ask about the fort, as one most probably will, one will be told of Babur's fascination for it, of Raja Man Singh Tomar (1486 - 1516) who lived there and who loved Mriganayani and music and of the Gwalior *gharana* that was born out of this love, of armies that attacked and of those that defended the citadel, and finally of the Scindias, who after conquering distant lands, spread at its feet a city adorned with palaces. All this may tempt one to return to Gwalior, to stay for a while, to see, learn and imbibe, for the city has a great deal more than its heat and its dust.

One cannot begin an account of the city with a flourish, for Gwalior does not permit itself to be moulded into a metaphor. Its structures and its arts, its traditions and its way of life do not blend and transform themselves into an identity. Each continues to live, as it was born, separately. One has therefore to begin at the beginning.

Over a thousand years ago, in the tenth century, Raja Suraj Sen, a Rajput chieftain from Kutwar, some forty kilometres north of Gwalior, while hunting, was separated from his followers. Climbing to the summit of the hill on which the fort now stands, he met the hermit, Gwalipa who offered him water from a nearby stream. When he drank the water a miracle occurred: he was cured of a skin disease that had afflicted him for years. In gratitude he asked the sage to name his reward, and was told to enlarge the spring, build a tank, and to make his headquarters on the hill. This he did, naming the hill Gwaliawar, a gift of Gwalia or Gwalipa. The large tank built by the Raja on the saint's advice, to store the miracle waters of the spring exists today as Suraj Kund.

The drive up the ramp that takes one to the crest of this hill is steep, as one rises 300 feet, past gigantic Jain *tirthankaras*, through five fortified gateways, till one reaches the plain above, stretching for two miles. On this are eight major tanks, six palaces, as many temples, a gurdwara and a public school. The magnificent outer walls of the fort still stand, three kilometres in length and thirty-five feet high, bearing witness to its reputation of being one of the most invincible forts in India.

If the fort dominates the city, then what crowns it is Man Mandir, the exquisite palace of Raja Man Singh Tomar. Babur, conqueror and an aesthete, who generally wrote disparagingly about what he saw in 'Hindostan', records that he was overwhelmed by the beauty of the palace – its gilded domes, white stuccoed walls, and the brilliant colours of its patterned tiles – blue, green, yellow and red – that border and add elegance to its walls. Like Babur, many have written about the palace, but those who visit it should cast all these descriptions aside, especially dry precise accounts like Cunningham's, and instead, walk around its halls like Jaswant Singh – descended from a family of guides – whose descriptions were just the right blend of fact and imagination to bring life to stone.

He began with Man Singh's pavilion, which took one ten centuries back to dark nights, when the rain fell gently and fireflies settled in hundreds on the wet tiles to provide a shimmering jewelled backdrop to evenings of music and dance. Below the pavilion are the royal chambers that looked ordinary enough till one heard Jaswant Singh's accounts of how they were cooled. Sandalwood fans, projecting out of the walls propelled air in, which was cooled and made fragrant by water in stone troughs. He then pointed to what appeared to be merely an ornamental stone screen above the beds, and showed behind it passages for light-footed maidens to run past, so that the sound of ankle bells woke the royal couple gently. The subterranean chambers housing the *zenana* were once lit by ingenious means, whereby sunlight would fall on mirrors strategically placed, to reflect into these rooms. Vast chambers with fine stone screens were once the music halls and behind these screens, the royal ladies would learn music from the great masters.

Then there are the subterranean cells which were the imperial prisons of the Mughals. Among those incarcerated were Aurangzeb's son Muhammad, his brother Murad and the sixth Sikh Guru, Hargobind Singh. Adjacent to Man Mandir are a cluster of medieval palaces – the

Vikramaditya Palace, Kirti Mandir, Shah Jahan Mahal and Jahangir Mahal. What are worth spending time on are Teli ka Mandir and Saas-Bahu ka Mandir.

The eighth-ninth century Teli ka Mandir is a Pratihara Vishnu temple which is a unique blend of architectural styles: the shape of the roof being distinctly Dravidian, and the decorative embellishments being typically north Indian. It is said that the temple was therefore called Telangana ka Mandir.

There are two versions regarding the origin of the name Saas-Bahu. The first is that the temples are named 'mother-in-law' and 'daughter-in-law', and the second is that the temples, dedicated to Vishnu, were called Sahasra Bahu. The temples were built by the Kachchapaghata king Mahipal around 1093. The larger temple has an intricately carved lotus ceiling.

Below Man Mandir, at the base of the hill, Raja Man Singh Tomar built yet another palace, Gujari Mahal for Mriganayani, the gazelle-eyed one. Legend has it that Raja Man Singh Tomar, on a hunting trip came across two buffaloes locked in battle, when out of nowhere a beautiful Gujjar woman, Mriganayani, came on the scene and separated them with her bare hands. Totally overwhelmed by her beauty and courage, the Raja asked her to be his queen. Mriganayani agreed, but set three conditions: she would never be in purdah, would accompany the Raja on his hunts, and would live in a separate palace, to which the waters of the Ravi which flowed past her village would be brought. The Raja erected Gujari Mahal and channelised the River Ravi through an aqueduct. The palace has open terraces where the royal couple enjoyed musical performances. From their love grew the Gwalior school of music, which is today the oldest of the *khayal gharanas* linking the 'formal structure and sacred intent of the *dhrupad* with the more personal and introspective idiom of the *khayal*.' Going back, one discovers that of the thirty-six singers and players who find mention in Abul Fazl's *Ain-i-Akbari*, fifteen had learnt their music in Gwalior. Amongst these was Miyan Tansen, a singer about whom Abul Fazl said, the like of him none had been heard in a thousand years. Beside his tomb Tansen Utsav is held every year – homage to both the singer and the city that remains one of the great centres of Indian classical music.

In the same enclosure as Tansen's tomb is a tomb of Muhammad Ghaus, a sixteenth century Muslim saint – the sides made of the most delicate lace-like stone screens. This is the famous Gwalior *jhilmili*, specimens of which still embellish many of the city's older houses. Walking down lanes like *Sarafa*, street of jewellers, you will suddenly catch a glimpse of these exquisite *jharokhas*, bringing grace to urban uncouthness. One of these finds place in Percy Brown's *History of Indian Architecture.*

There is little else to hold one's interest in the town, a concrete confusion that grew out of the camp of the Scindias. Mahadji Scindia spent most of his life in battle, and his armies under the command of Benoit de Boigne swept all before them, defeating

the forces of the Rajputs, the Holkars and even Delhi, and reinstating the Emperor Shah Alam in 1785. It was not until 1810 that Daulat Rao Scindia permanently fixed his headquarters at Gwalior. So even today, the town, parts of which are called Lashkar and Campoo — associations of forces and camp — retain the ruggedness and bustle of an army on the move, till one enters the placidity and the spaciousness of the roads that lead to, and the gardens that surround Jai Vilas, palace of the Scindias.

ABOVE

Jai Vilas Palace, Gwalior.

There is nothing to remind one of the camp in this immense ivory-coloured structure that rises and spreads itself in stately symmetry. Designed by Lt Col Sir Michael Filose, the palace is a fine fusion of Tuscan and Corinthian architecture. Wandering through its large halls one gets the feel of royal living because, unlike other palaces

open to the public which are mere carcasses of a once glorious past, Jai Vilas is a palace where one of India's great princes still lives.

Most significant of all is the Darbar Hall, a colossal chamber with ceilings painted with melted gold weighing approximately 560 kgs, heavy draperies, rare Persian carpets, the floor covered with perhaps the world's largest one-piece carpet woven in situ, and antique French and Italian furniture. Dominating the room are the gigantic cut glass chandeliers, weighing three and a half tons each; it is said that these were hung only after ten elephants had tested the strength of the roof!

The old retainer taking you around has a fund of stories that transport you, swiftly and totally, into a past that was literally another world – of the viceroys and princes who stayed there, and the ceremonies, banquets and *shikar*s that were so much a part of their lives.

The palace has a collection of English Chippendale, exquisite Persian carpets, French and Italian furniture and quaint items, including a silver train that ran on miniature rails on the banquet hall table, with cut-glass wagons, carrying after-dinner Cognac and cigars.

LEFT

The luxurious reception room of Jai Vilas Palace, Gwalior.

ABOVE

The Maharajah of Gwalior, Madhav Rao Scindia I (1886 – 1925).

RIGHT

The Scindia chhatris *(cenotaphs) in Shivpuri are exquisitely carved.*

But if the palace is linked with the people, it is not through pomp and pageantry, but memories of a ruler who cared for his subjects. Madhav Rao Scindia I, on his investiture in 1886, sent a message to his people, which read:

> For the future my care will be to improve in every way the conditions of life of the poorest of my people, to ensure that justice is dispensed to my subjects independently and without delay, to protect them by the efficiency of the police, to place within the reach of all, the advantages of a good education and medical relief and to develop in every way, the trade and industries of my state. My great desire is that my people should know me as their friend and I hope, after a short time, to travel throughout my whole state so that I may get to know my people in person, may hear of their difficulties and their wants, and may learn by seeing them in their homes and at their work, how best I and my Government may help them to prosperity and happiness.

A truly remarkable message from a remarkable ruler, who then strove, throughout his reign, to fulfill these promises. A glance at the many volumes of his *Policy Durbar*, manuals of administration, cannot fail to impress, not only by the range of subjects dealt with but equally by the precision of presentation and depth of treatment. Much of what he did was quite unique, like setting apart a substantial part of the state's revenues for funding irrigation, education and famine relief, constructing a large number of irrigation dams, developing the Gwalior Light Railway, starting factories with state encouragement, setting up the first state department of archaeology, and providing the finest of secular traditions by building a temple, a gurdwara, a mosque and a theosophical lodge in his gardens. True to his promise, he toured extensively, and even though he was a twenty-one-gun salute, full-blooded Maharajah, he used to run upstairs carrying his own *bastas* (bags). Madhav Rao was a legend in his lifetime and became to his people their friend, as he wanted to be. It is no wonder that Madho Maharaj is, even today, both venerated and loved by the people of Gwalior.

So this in brief is Gwalior. But what in fact do citadel and palace, craft and music, add up to? The city lacks the cultivated charm of Lucknow, the aristocratic ageing grace of Kolkata or the stately symmetry of Lutyen's Delhi. The attractions of Gwalior fail to fuse, and the city is bereft of an essence. Yet, its citizens are saved from the triviality of a small-town existence by the fact of communication between the masses and their monuments, the palace and the people.

These complex strands of interaction are what provide to those who grow up and live in this city, something precious and rare today – a character that is distinct.

Shivpuri | Situated 112 kilometres from Gwalior is the town of Shivpuri, the summer capital, and the *shikar* grounds of the Scindias, which has much to bring back flavours of their times.

Abul Fazl informs us that in 1584, Emperor Akbar returning from the kingdom of Malwa captured a large herd of elephants in the forests of Sipri (Shivpuri), so the forests must have had an abundance of wildlife. However, what attracted the Maharajahs most, was the tiger. At the turn of the last century, the state was divided into *shikargah*s or hunting preserves, many of which were reserved for the sole use of the ruler.

Shivpuri was one such *shikargah*, the major hunting preserve of the Scindias. There is a fine shooting box that still remains, built out from the wall of the Chand Patha dam. The ruler and guests would arrive by boat across the river, enter the box, and sit and await the tiger. As the night wore on, the tiger would move to the bait, being viewed with ease with the assistance of great arc lamps, get photographed, and then shot! It was all rather leisurely and grand.

A stone slab between the 101st and 102nd milestone on the Gwalior-Mumbai road has on it engraved, that on the 11 April 1914, His Excellency, the Right Honourable Charles Baron Hardinge of Penhurst, shot a tiger measuring eleven feet six and ¾ inches. The story goes, in all probability apocryphal, that in the Gwalior tape used to measure slain tigers, every foot had eleven inches!

When the hunting privileges of rulers were taken away, the area lost its protection and wildlife was ruthlessly exterminated. To prevent further destruction the area was protected, being declared Madhav National Park in 1958.

With dry mixed deciduous forests and flat grasslands it is essentially a deer park, large carnivores being rare or absent. Most easily sighted are the Chinkara (Indian gazelle), the small delicate antelope which stands motionless, staring at the intruder, and then bounds away, and the Chital (Spotted deer), the gregarious deer, reddish-brown in colour, flecked with white spots. Other species found include Nilgai (Blue bull), Sambar, Chausinga (Four-horned antelope), Blackbuck, Sloth bear (occasionally seen, usually nocturnal), Wild boar and the Common langur.

The national park is rich in avifauna and mainly known for migratory waterfowl that arrive from Siberia to winter on and around the lakes. A particularly good site for viewing is where the forest track crosses the wide rocky stream that flows from the waste weir. Here one can spot Red-wattled lapwing, Large pied wagtails, Pond herons and often a White-breasted kingfisher. The birds include Painted storks, White ibises, egrets, teals, kingfishers, sandgrouses and at least seventy-five other varieties. Other faunal groups include the Marsh crocodile and the Indian python.

The *chhatris*, the marble cenotaphs of the Scindias, are a blend of Hindu and Islamic architecture, amidst formal gardens, within which life-size statues of the rulers are tended to by ceremonially dressed retainers, who lay flowers and incense before them. In the evenings, artistes offer classical melodies sitting before the statues.

ABOVE

Detail of fine inlay work on a marble chhatri *in Shivpuri.*

In the forest park there is a quaint structure of a small castle, built by Jiyaji Rao Scindia for George V who was visiting on a tiger shoot. It offers an attractive view of the lake. Equally unusual is the Sakhya Sagar Boat Club on the lake with a magnificent view. Also worth visiting is the Madhav Vilas, the summer palace of the Scindias and the Collectorate, where Tantia Tope was hanged.

Shivpuri is a pleasant experience for those visiting Gwalior, a green and pleasant retreat retaining the flavours of royalty.

Orchha | The sixteenth century town of Orchha lies 128 kilometres south of Gwalior.

The literal meaning of Orchha is hidden treasure. It certainly is one of India's most precious gems. The magic of Orchha lies in its magnificent palaces and exquisite temples, set in sweeping, undulating terrain, with forests around, and the lovely winding River Betwa below.

Orchha is not a monument, nor even a group of monuments, but an entire

ABOVE

A view of Chaturbhuj Temple, Orchha, at dusk.

medieval city, much of which remains what it was, embellished with the most delightful legends. Founded in 1531 by Raja Rudra Pratap, it served as the capital of the Bundela rulers till they moved to Tikamgarh in 1738.

When you stay in Sheesh Mahal, a palace converted into a hotel by M.P. Tourism, and look out from some of its many windows, each view is a framed medieval painting, with nothing to remind you of the twenty-first century.

The legends of Orchha commence with the inception of the dynasty. It is said that in the eleventh century, a Rajput prince offered himself as a sacrifice to the mountain goddess Vindhyavasini, who, pleased with the prince's devotional fervour, intervened and named him *Bundela* (one who offered blood).

Centuries later, Raja Bir Singh (1602 - 1627) had a somewhat different offering for his friend, Salim who later became Emperor Jahangir. Knowing of Salim's dislike for Abul Fazl, who was also Akbar's very close confidant chronicler, and military commander, he planned his murder in 1602. It is said that when Abul Fazl was forewarned of the plot, his response was, "I am a General of the imperial army, so how can anyone touch me?" Touched he was, indeed set upon, and brutally murdered by tribesmen near Antri.

When Salim ascended the throne as Jahangir, Bir Singh, with his close proximity to the Emperor, was naturally invested with great power. Jahangir did stop once at Orchha, immediately after which the palace where he stayed was named Jahangir Mahal.

The building, perhaps the finest example of Bundela architecture in the country, has 236 chambers around a central courtyard, embellished with glazed tiles and delicate *jaalis*, with a skyline dominated by *chhatris*, cupolas and domes. A fine view of the palace can be had from Sheesh Mahal, which adjoins it. Massive, masculine and severe, as a structure it cannot fail to evoke awe.

Opposite Jahangir Mahal is Raj Mahal, built by Bir Singh's predecessor Madhukar Shah (1554 - 1592). Being deeply religious, he had the walls decorated with exquisite murals on a variety of religious themes.

Rai Praveen Mahal, another palace, was the abode of Rai Praveen, poetess and musician lover of Raja Indramani (1672 - 1675). News of her beauty reached the imperial court at Delhi, and Emperor Akbar sent for her. Since her lover and royal master was in no position to protect her from so formidable an opponent, she had perforce to rely on her wits. She sent to the Emperor a message in verse,

> *Crows and dogs and scavengers feed on food left over by others.*
> *Of what breed are you My Lord?*

Akbar impressed, had her returned to Orchha.

ABOVE

Entrance to the Rama Raja Temple, Orchha.

RIGHT

A priest sitting outside a temple, Orchha.

The Rama Raja Temple also has a tale behind it. Madhukar Shah's wife, Ganesh Kunwari, after a dream of Lord Rama visiting her, journeyed to Ayodhya and brought a statue of the Lord. Since the temple where it was to be installed was not ready, it was placed in the palace. But, alas the queen had forgotten the injunction she received at Ayodha, that the idol would have to be enshrined at the spot where it touched the ground; and so it remained in the palace since it could not be moved. It is therefore the only shrine in the country where Rama is worshipped as a king, and to this day the entrance to the sanctum has armed guards on either side.

Dinman Hardaul's Palace is yet another place with a legend. Hardaul, son of Raja Bir Singh Ju Deo, led an unblemished saintly life. When suspected of having a relationship with the consort of his elder brother Jhujhar, he took his own life. He is, over centuries, worshipped as a god in many villages in Bundelkhand.

An equally pious person was Jhujhar's son, Dhurjban, who embraced Islam when he married a Muslim, and spent the latter part of his life in prayer. He is worshipped as a *pir* today.

Other places to be visited are Shahid Smarak, built in memory of freedom fighter Chandrashekhar Azad, who lived in hiding, and worked here from 1926 - 1927; the fourteen *chhatris* of the rulers; the Lakshminarayana Temple, containing the most exquisite of Orchha's wall paintings, which include scenes from the mutiny of 1857; Chaturbhuj Temple; and Phool Bagh, what must have been a gem of a Mughal garden with the added attraction of a subterranean retreat.

A visit to Orchha is truly memorable, a place where Nature, man's creations, and legends of gods blend most perfectly.

BHOPAL - BHOJPUR - BHIMBETKA - SANCHI - UDAIGIRI - UDAYPUR - PACHMARHI

Bhopal | For those who have not visited the city, the image conjured up at the mention of Bhopal will most probably be that of one of the many railway stations passed by in a long train journey, or of one of India's numerous dusty crowded towns, with nondescript, functional architecture.

A less prosaic and more tragic association is that of the gas disaster of 1984, when 40 tons of methyl isocyanate leaked out killing 3,000 - 8,000 people in the first instance, and another 6,000 - 23,000 over the years, depending on whether you believe in official figures or those cited by NGOs.

What one does see therefore, comes as a very pleasant surprise.

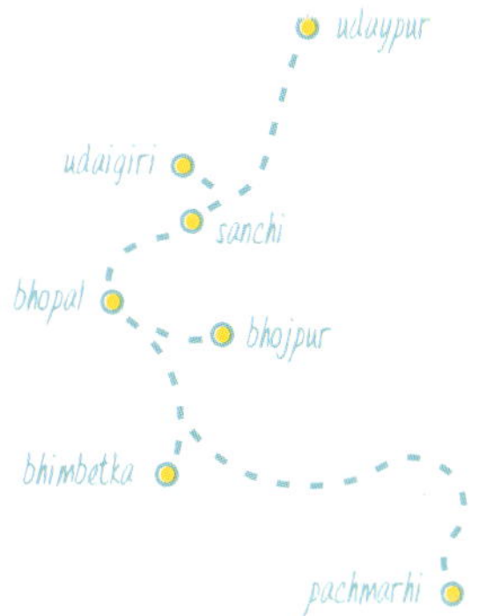

LEFT

Shimmering reflections of the sunset on Bada Talab, Bhopal.

Bhopal is known as the city of lakes, and it is lakes that greet one on arrival. The road from the railway station crosses the Chhota Talab (Lower Lake) and if one flies in, then the drive into town skirts the Bada Talab (Great Lake), spanning thirty-one kilometres; more like an expanse of the sea than a lake, which while enveloping the city, reflects it as well. The saying goes, *Tal to tal Bhopal tal, aur sab talaiya.* However dominant the Great Lake is, it is only one of the many. Next only in beauty to and complementing the lakes is the undulating body of the city spread over three hills – Idgah, Shamla and Ahmedabad. The city never tires, because the ups and downs bring so much variety.

Bhopal is over a thousand years old, if we link it with the city built by Raja Bhoj (1010 - 1055). The modern city, however, was developed by that Afghan soldier of fortune, Dost Mohammad (1708 - 1740). Straying from the imperial Mughal armies, using military strategy and treachery with equal skill, always backed by enormous courage, he exploited internal dissensions to find a kingdom.

His first capital was Islamnagar, eleven kilometres from Bhopal. The story goes that, posing as a rich visiting nobleman, he set up camp, and invited the ruler of Jagdishpur to a meal. After the guests settled, on an agreed signal, the ropes of the tent were cut, after which they were swiftly slaughtered and their bodies thrown into a river, which came to be known as 'Halali'. The gardens, fountains and palaces that remain give no clue about these bloody beginnings. Dost Mohammad also befriended the Gond queen of Bhopal, and after her death took over the kingdom.

New Bhopal was created in the mid-fifties, as the capital of the state of Madhya Pradesh. It therefore had a semblance of town planning with geometrically laid out wide roads, government offices and residences, but was in danger of having a profile of excessive functionalism, had it not been for the efforts of some imaginative officers who worked hard to prevent this. Stark structures of brick and mortar were mellowed by gardens and flowers, and open spaces created into parks, planned with great care, using contours for beds and streams, and rocks as contrasts to pastel shades. Bhopal became a city of gardens.

Successive administrators also had the foresight to invite some of the brightest and the best of India's private architects to design public buildings, the most outstanding examples of which are the exquisite Bharat Bhavan and the monumental Vidhan Bhavan designed by Charles Correa, for which he received the Agha Khan award.

What is also unusual is the use of the banks of the Great Lake to house not government offices or residences of the powerful or affluent, but unique public institutions.

When the Government of India was setting up the National Museum of Man, it was persuaded that Bhopal, which borders one of the richest prehistoric sites (Bhimbetka) in the country, would be an appropriate location. Covering an area of over 200

acres, the museum has replicas of dwelling units of tribal, coastal and mountain people from all over the country, with an informative closed door gallery.

Close by is Bharat Bhavan, a uniquely designed complex which houses an art gallery, with fine exhibits of contemporary, folk and tribal paintings; a workshop for the fine arts; a repertory theatre; indoor and outdoor auditoria; libraries of Indian poetry, classical and folk music and the largest collection of tribal artefacts in the world. This unique institution, the sensitivity to, and love of all art forms by the people of Bhopal, and the creative efforts of the Government of Madhya Pradesh together led Prime Minister Indira Gandhi to describe Bhopal as the cultural capital of India, a city to which many eminent painters, poets and playwrights came to settle, including J. Swaminathan, Habib Tanvir and B.V. Karanth.

ABOVE

Entrance to Taj-ul-Masajid, Bhopal, the second largest mosque in Asia.

Also located on the shores of the Great Lake is Van Vihar, where a very large variety of animals live in luxuriant natural surroundings, spread over 1,000 acres, in the finest zoo in India.

Madhya Pradesh, due to its rivers, fertility of soils, having all major trade routes passing through it, and being south of the areas that marauding armies reached, has an enormous wealth of superb structures and sculptures in an excellent state of preservation. The State Archeological Museum, located on Shamla Hills, bordering the Great Lake, houses a rich collection of sculptures with some rare exhibits such as Alakshmi, an almost modern depiction of poverty; the Panchamukhi Ganesha, and the valuable reproductions of the Bagh frescoes by Asit Haldar, Nandlal Bose and Sarkis Katchadourian, the originals unfortunately now in a very poor state of preservation.

Despite these efforts, New Bhopal, like New Delhi, being an artificially created planned city, suffers from the absence of character that results only from organic growth, for which, like Old Delhi, we have to go to Old Bhopal. The heart of the old city is the 'Chowk', its winding lanes lined with shops selling beadwork bags, bell metal objects and silver jewellery. Spread over the old city are the palaces and mosques built by the Begums of Bhopal, rulers who displayed a range of very unusual talents.

Qudsia Begum succeeded her husband at the age of eighteen and ruled from 1819 to 1837. Though illiterate, she refused to permit the purdah system, and had the strength to declare her two-year-old daughter Sikandar her successor. She constructed the Jama Masjid and Gohar Mahal, a delightful little palace overlooking the Great Lake.

Sikandar Begum not only followed her mother in not observing purdah, but went a step further and took to the martial arts! Her enthusiasm was however not confined to gender issues; she was proactive in education, opening schools and madrasas, and also constructed the Moti Masjid and Moti Mahal.

The only surviving child of Sikandar Begum (1844 - 1860), Shah Jahan (1868 - 1901), was perhaps the most remarkable of the Begums. Following the fine traditions of her predecessors she showed keen interest in schemes related to the welfare of her subjects. Like her namesake at Delhi, she was also a great builder – constructing a mini-city named Shahjahanabad after her, initiating the construction of the magnificent Taj-ul-Masajid (Crown of Mosques), the second largest in Asia and a score of other buildings. Both learned and religious, she authored several books in Urdu, donated to a mosque at Woking, Surrey in England and to the Muhammad Anglo-Oriental College which later led to the founding of the Aligarh Muslim University.

Her daughter Sultan Jahan Begum who succeeded her, built Sadar Manzil, Qauser-e-Sultani (currently housing Safia College) and Noor-us-Sabah (now a splendid heritage hotel), and was the first Chancellor of Aligarh Muslim University.

Bhopal therefore has the charm and aroma of a medieval Islamic city with its palaces, mosques and winding lanes.

More recently Begum Sajida Sultan, daughter of Nawab Hamidullah Khan, the last ruling Nawab of Bhopal, married Nawab Iftekhar Ali Khan of Pataudi who captained the Indian cricket team. As an interesting aside, his son Mansoor Ali Khan, the present Nawab also followed his footsteps. He married Sharmila Tagore, the famous film actor. This was a union of two important royal families.

Another fascinating connection was the one between Bhopal and the Bourbons. It is said that Jean Philippe de Bourbon-Navarre arrived at the court of Emperor Akbar in 1560. In 1739 when Nadir Shah sacked Delhi the Bourbons moved to Gwalior, Salvador-de-Bourbon being appointed *Kiledar* of Gwalior Fort. The Marathas under Mahadji Scindia captured the fort and imprisoned the Bourbons. Salvador then moved to Bhopal where he was not only welcomed and given land, but came to be popularly known as the *Inayat Masih*.

ABOVE

A gateway leading to the Chowk in the old city of Bhopal.

ABOVE

A portrait of the remarkable Begum of Bhopal, Shah Jahan.

RIGHT

Devotees offering fruits and flowers to the shivlinga *at Bhojeshwar Temple, Bhojpur.*

His son Shahzad Masih was a scholar, fluent in Urdu and Persian, a military strategist and organiser. Presently, Balthazar Napoleon de Bourbon who lives in Bhopal is said to possess a strong claim to the French throne!

The city, on its own merits a stay of at least a day or two, but, more importantly, it is also the gateway to the extraordinary sites of Bhojpur and Bhimbetka, and to Sanchi and Pachmarhi.

Bhojpur - Bhimbetka | Bhojpur and Bhimbetka can both be visited in a day. Setting off early, one can drive to Bhimbetka, breakfast there, drive back via Bhojpur and return to Bhopal in time for lunch.

Bhimbetka, forty-seven kilometres from Bhopal, spread over twenty-five square kilometres, has the largest collection of prehistoric rock shelter paintings in India, and is a site which has been Man's abode for lakhs of years. Of the several hundred caves having paintings, those open to visitors are a little over a dozen.

The paintings, ranging from prehistoric times to the early historic, often superimposed on each other, depict the myriad aspects of Man's life – hunting, riding, fighting, drinking, dancing, praying – and a range of animals, which are best viewed at the Zoo Rock which depicts elephants, Sambar, Bison, deer, peacocks and snakes, as well as hunting scenes with bows, arrows, swords and shields.
The paintings are stylised, often reflecting human emotions, the Bison being hunted looks enormous before minuscule human beings. Quite unique is the depiction of a pregnant deer, showing the calf in the stomach!

Most striking are the vibrant colours which have survived all these years; they blaze into life when water is sprayed on them. Even for those who may not find these paintings interesting, the massive bizarre-shaped black rocks, amidst forests, are themselves a visual treat.

As extraordinary as the site was its discoverer — V.S.Wakankar. Wakankar had, as a young man, developed a passionate interest in rock shelter paintings, and visited most of these sites in India on his own resources, travelling by train, bus and on foot. One day, while on a train from Bhopal to Hoshangabad, he saw formations that he suspected were rock shelters; discontinuing his train journey, he walked to the hills later to be named Bhimbetka, to discover one of the richest group of rock shelter paintings in the world, now inscribed by UNESCO as a World Heritage Site. Wakankar's labours and accomplishments gained him international recognition amongst scholars of prehistory.

Returning from Bhimbetka, and taking a short diversion, one reaches Bhojpur, home to the great Shaivite Bhojeshwar Temple, constructed by the legendary Raja Bhoj — warrior, scholar and patron of the arts. The approach to the monument has remains of the embankments of the enormous lake, said to be 250 square kilometres in area, built by Raja Bhoj, which was later destroyed by Hoshang Shah (1400 - 1435).

Gond legends state that it took Hoshang Shah's army three months to destroy the dam (which was built on the lake) and three years to empty the lake, altering the climate of the region.

The incomplete temple can be sighted from a distance, but what you see on entering can never be anticipated – the gigantic *shivlinga*, 7.5 feet in height, with a circumference of 17.8 feet, on a massive platform 21.5 square feet – a great symbol of life-force, a sight compelling reverence. Due to Raja Bhoj's involvements in wars, the temple remained incomplete; but still remains one of the best examples of temple architecture of its times. Outside are half-finished sculptures, the earthen ramp used to lift stones to the *shikhara* (spire) of the temple, and architectural designs of the temple engraved in the rocks. It appears as if the workers have just broken off – and the scene remained frozen for over 900 years.

ABOVE

Bhimbetka rock paintings.

RIGHT

The Great Stupa at Sanchi.

Sanchi - Udaigiri - Udaypur

Sanchi, a World Heritage Site, lies forty-six kilometres from Bhopal. The monument and the area surrounding it, exudes an air of tranquility, which perhaps explains why it was chosen by Emperor Ashoka for construction of the best known of his stupas. It was here that he met Devi, daughter of a merchant from Vidisha, whom he married, and when years later their son Mahendra visited his mother, she took him up to the monastery she had built.

Though not directly connected with the life of the Buddha, the monuments, amongst the most well preserved in the country, depict the birth, development and decay of Buddhist art and architecture, over a period of thirteen hundred years, from the third century BC to twelfth century AD; the stone casing of the stupa being constructed by the Sungas, and the balustrade and the *toranas* (gateways) by the Satavahanas. There was revival of construction during the Guptas, and thereafter the monument

remained in oblivion till it was discovered in 1818 by an Englishman, General Taylor. Paradoxically, it was not mentioned by the seventh century Chinese traveller Hiuen Tsang, the purpose of whose incredibly long journeys was to visit Buddhist monuments.

Thereafter there was considerable vandalism by treasure hunters, and damage by amateur archaeologists, including Capt Johnson, Assistant Political Agent in Bhopal in 1822 and Alexander Cunningham in 1851.

Systematic preservation only commenced in 1904 under the direction of John Marshall, Director General, Archaeological Survey of India. The PWD rest house has albums of excellent photographs of the remains exposed during Marshall's time.

The dome of the Great Stupa at Sanchi, said to symbolise the cosmic mountain, conveys through its simple and benign form, a message of peace. It is crowned by the *chhattravali*, the *triratnas* representing the three pillars of Buddhism – the Buddha, the Dharma and the Sangha. Providing contrast to the serenity, are the scenes from the *Jataka* tales carved on the

ABOVE

Carvings on toranas, *Sanchi.*

toranas which depict the hustle and bustle of everyday life. These renderings on stone are intricate and very fine, being crafted by the ivory workers of Vidisha, and display in a continuous form, rather like a cinema reel, the *Jataka* tales and important events in the life of the Buddha, such as Maya's dream and conception, the Four Drives, the Great Departure, Enlightenment, the First Sermon and Decease. In these depictions, the Buddha never appears in person, but is symbolised through a horse without a rider, an umbrella over a throne, the Bodhi tree and footprints of the Great Master.

The stupa and its gateways represent a stage in Indian art form when creativity flowed, unrestrained by orthodox canons and represented a joy in, and celebration of, life in all its forms; bird, beast, plant and man merging continuously, and ever so naturally, into each other. Stupa three contains relics of two of Buddha's disciples, Sariputra and Maudgalyayana, discovered by Alexander Cunningham. There are two temples in the precincts – Temple 18, built in the seventh century, and Temple 17 belonging to the Gupta period – representing the development of temple architecture in India.

Close to Sanchi, three kilometres from the town of Vidisha is a somewhat unique monument, Heliodorus's Pillar, which proclaims the conversion of the Greek ambassador to Vaishnavism in 140 BC, unusual because the Indian tradition was the opposite – absorbing the faiths of those who came.

Also close by are the Udaigiri caves, which contain fine specimens of sculptures of the golden age of the Guptas. What is stunning is the statue of Varaha (one of the incarnations of Lord Vishnu); massive, bearing the delicate *prithvi* (earth) on his tusk, representing the confident might of the imperial Guptas and their capacity to uplift what is considered precious.

All this is a feast enough, but you cannot leave without visiting Udaypur or Udayeshwar, which has the exquisite eleventh century Neelkantheshvara Temple, believed to be the finest specimen of northern Indian medieval temple architecture.

Pachmarhi

Go find a road that runs out to the sky
Away from the noise of the street.
Go find a hill where the big winds sweep by
And green grasses blow at your feet.
Go seek a place where the Kingfishers swoop
Some haunt where the quiet waters gleam.
Go seek a bank where the willow trees stoop
Over the brink of a stream.
In the green silences life seems so good
Here all your questionings cease.
For the husk at the heart of a bird-haunted wood
Gives you a sense of God's Peace.

– Patience Strong

In 1857, following the rioting, Capt J. Forsyth of the Bengal Lancers was sent to report on the

area of the dense Satpura jungles. Heading a column of troops, after walking for twenty-seven kilometres, he came upon the plateau. He wrote, "Altogether, the aspect of the plateau was much more that of a fine English park than of any scene I had before come across in India."

Forsyth's note and description of Pachmarhi led Sir Richard Temple, Chief Commissioner to send him back to examine the possibility of using it, which ultimately resulted in the establishment of a sanatorium. It later became a centre for the Army Education Corps and the Army Music School.

The flowing meadows, in the heart of Pachmarhi, and its tranquility, still remain its central appeal.

Pachmarhi is not merely another hill station: viewed thus it would be the poor man's Mussoorie or Shimla, since it is only 3,500 feet high and not close to, or surrounded by, the Himalayas. It does however possess a variety of attractions that are quite unique.

To begin with, for many years it remained unchanged and unspoilt, with vast tranquil meadows, long quiet walks including the 'Short Chukker' and the 'Long Chukker', and a number of very quaint nineteenth century cottages and churches, all of which add up to give it a picture book charm and the pleasures of a genuine retreat.

The appeal of Pachmarhi also lies in the fact that, unlike most hill stations that have, at most, half a dozen spots or walks, Pachmarhi has well over fifty. Since the majority of these are streams, falls and pools, deep down in its valleys, reaching these is strenuous, but once having done so, one cannot but be mesmerised by their magic. Even at the height of summer these streams, with delicate leafy forests and ferns as backdrops, are ice-cold. One is told that the British used to place mangoes and beer bottles at one end, spend hours swimming and scrambling, and retrieve these downstream, totally chilled! The spots were given charming names by the British: Saunder's Pool, Dorothy Deep, Fairy Pool, Bee Falls, and Piccadilly.

Pachmarhi is also a destination for pilgrims. The Pandava caves, which though said to be Buddhist, are associated with the Pandavas; and Mahadeo, Jata Shankar and Chauragarh, are other landmarks which are associated with Lord Shiva. For the elderly and less adventurous, the views from Dhoopgarh (Sunset Point) and Handi Khoh, with its sheer 300 foot drop, are breathtaking.

One of the descriptions of Madhya Pradesh in the seventies was, 'undiscovered, unhurried and unspoilt'. This may still be true of Pachmarhi, if visited in off-season.

LEFT

A rock face in Pachmarhi; such natural formations are an invitation to rock climbers.

JABALPUR - KANHA

Jabalpur | To most tourists Jabalpur is not a destination, but merely a point of access, a railway station or an airport for Kanha, arguably the country's finest wildlife sanctuary. What are presented by tourist guides, more or less as 'add ons', are the Marble Rocks, and places to visit such as Madan Mahal fort, the Chausath Yogini Temple, and the museum; but as is the case with so much else in Madhya Pradesh, Jabalpur has a lot more to offer than what meets the eye.

Let us start with some 'add ons'.

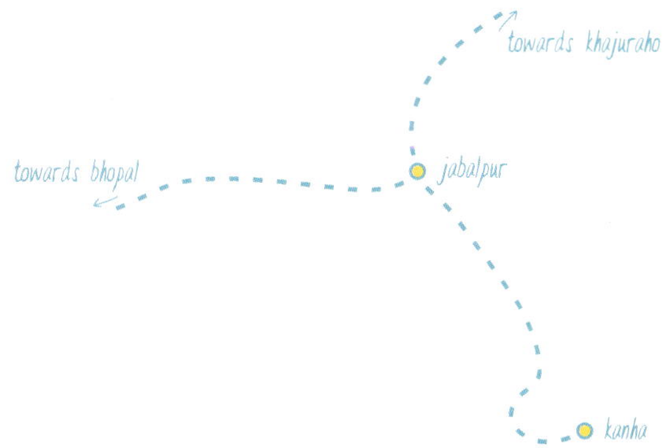

LEFT

The majestic Marble Rocks on the River Narmada in Jabalpur.

The visit to Marble Rocks is a unique experience. Here the Narmada flows between sheer white cliffs that rise dramatically over a hundred feet on either side. This is what Capt J. Forsyth wrote about it, in the middle of the nineteenth century, in his book, *Highlands of Central India*:

> The eye never wearies of the...effect produced by the broken and reflected sunlight, now glancing from a pinnacle of snow-white marble reared against the deep blue of the sky as from a point of silver; touching here and there with bright lights the prominence of the middle heights; and again losing itself in soft grayish blue of their recesses. Here and there the white saccharine limestone is seamed by veins of dark green or black volcanic rock; a contrast which only enhances like a setting of jet, the purity of the surrounding marble.

Almost a hundred and fifty years later, the late poet Dom Moraes in his travel book on Madhya Pradesh, *Answered by Flutes* wrote:

> Outside the city the Narmada makes a broad, blue, rippled streak between high, wrinkled cliffs of pure white marble. At certain times of day the light takes the marble and stipples it with shades of turquoise and pink: this is observable if you take a boat out on the river, the Narmada lapping past the bows as you pass the raw material for thousands of statues...

Visit it you must, by boat, if possible by moonlight, to drink in one of Nature's gifts, quite unlike any other, and then on to Dhuandhar, the misty falls, for an experience you will always cherish.

Next in the itinerary would perhaps be the Rani Durgavati Museum, which, apart from the range and variety of exhibits (Jabalpur's history dates back to the *Mahabharata*, in which it finds mention as 'Tripuri') has a fine collection of sculptures and inscriptions of the Kalachuris of Tripuri. Tripuri incidentally was the name the Congress gave its session held in 1939, made historic by the fact that Subhash Chandra Bose was re-elected President, against the wishes of Mahatma Gandhi. What would have added to the museum, but which are unfortunately not there, are sections devoted to two remarkable persons, with nothing in common, save their association with Jabalpur, their passion, and their courage – Rani Durgavati and Sir William Henry Sleeman.

Madhya Pradesh is fortunate in having had some remarkable women rulers; Rani Ahilyabai Holkar of Maheshwar/Indore, the Begums of Bhopal and Rani Durgavati of Jabalpur.

On the death of her husband in 1548, Rani Durgavati took up the reins of the Gond kingdom. Said to be both beautiful and compassionate, she also displayed extraordinary martial prowess and valour. In 1556, when Baz Bahadur of Mandu attacked her, he suffered a humiliating defeat and fled from the battlefield. Thereafter Baz Bahadur renounced arms forever, concentrating solely on his lovely consort Rupmati, music and song. This is one of history's ironies, in that it is the memories of their love of music and each other that provides to Mandu its flavour and its magic!

When eight years later, Asaf Khan, sent by Emperor Akbar, attacked the Gond kingdom, Rani Durgavati once again donned armour and led her armies to battle, riding on an elephant. Injured twice by arrows, she is said to have asked her mahout to have her trampled by the elephant, and when he refused, stabbed herself. She remains an inspiration to people in this region.

Very different, but equally a source of inspiration, was William Henry Sleeman. Born in 1778 in Cornwall, which has some of the most beautiful countryside in England, Sleeman, from his youth had dreams of joining the army and going to India; he studied Arabic and Hindustani before recruitment, and later Persian and Gorkhali. In those days the Indian Civil Service and the Indian Army were, for Englishmen, amongst the finest of professions – both a calling and an honour. After arriving at Calcutta (now Kolkata), Sleeman, whilst pursing his career, studied Indian culture and Hinduism. In 1816 Dr Robert Sherwood, a scholar on Hinduism wrote an article in the *Madras Literary Gazette* on the phenomenon existing over the ages, of large numbers of 'native' travellers mysteriously disappearing while journeying. He wrote about the operations of *phansigar*s or stranglers, or thugs, as they were known in northern India, operating under a cult to murder travellers. Their modus operandi was to befriend and persuade travellers to journey together for safety, and at an opportune moment, strangle them with sashes. This was all part of an elaborate ritual, connected with Goddess Kali, knowledge of which was passed down the generations. Thugs did not of course desist from plunder, so, as is the case with so many practises, purported to propitiate the gods, there was a strong underlying economic motive as well.

Most Englishmen who came across the article kept it aside, feeling it was concerned with an obscure custom that affected only natives, having no connection with their lives. But Sleeman was one Englishman who read the article, understood the critical seriousness of the subject, and, what is most important, decided to do something about it. He applied for a transfer from the army to the civil service and was appointed Junior Assistant Magistrate in 1820 at Saugor (now Sagar). When he was elevated two years later as Magistrate of Narsinghpur, having the police under his control, he was in a position to act. His first efforts were to gather information on the cult, which he did assiduously. He found that the practice, which was hereditary, having prevailed for hundreds of years, centering around worship of Kali, resulted in 30,000 - 40,000 deaths a year, victims being dumped into pre-prepared mass graves. It enjoyed the patronage of local rulers and bankers, and its members were otherwise respected members of their societies. After acquiring detailed knowledge of the practice, he embarked upon a mission to eradicate it, travelling and camping for many weeks of every month, braving snakes, leeches, mosquitoes, rains, dust and the searing heat, always accompanied by his young French wife Am, who was smitten by the same zeal for the task. All this weakened Sleeman physically, who in his early forties was afflicted with malaria and rheumatism.

Nevertheless, by 1838, Sleeman had captured and tried 3,266 thugs, and by 1840 - 41, after hundreds of years, there was for the first time in India, no reports of strangled travellers. The menace of thugs had been totally eliminated. The people of the region gratefully remembered him and all he did by naming a town after him — Sleemanabad. In 1856 he and his wife sailed for England looking forward to his well-deserved retirement in his beloved Cornwall: but all that was not to be, because he died of heart failure only nine days after landing. His life is a demonstration of what can be achieved by a single person, possessing passion, courage and integrity.

Jabalpur, which was an important city in the British administered Mahakoshal region, retained both memories and many of the fine traditions of the Indian Civil Service. The house once occupied by Sleeman became the official residence of the Commissioner, Jabalpur. Years later, R.C.V.P. Noronha, posted as Commissioner, Jabalpur, lived there. One of the finest civil servants produced by India in the last century, Noronha used to take young probationers of the Indian Administrative Service to a stone on which is engraved the names of British civil servants, who died, most of them, very young, while working in relief work, a fitting memorial to their dedication and zeal.

The larger towns of British administered territories like, Poona, Allahabad and Jabalpur, retained an old-world charm with their picturesque avenues, dignified bungalows, shopping areas, clubs and educational institutions, all amidst luxurious stretches of spaces and greens. Towns like Jabalpur were good places to grow up in, with fine schools and colleges, dedicated teachers, and a leisurely pace of life that permitted civilised social interactions. It is no wonder that many of the country's best doctors, lawyers, judges and civil servants, came from this town.

Kanha

Wood and Water. Wind and Tree,
Wisdom, Strength and Courtesy,
Jungle — favour go with thee.

— Rudyard Kipling

Situated 176 kilometres from Jabalpur, Kanha National Park has an unmatched splendour of its own. To begin with, its spread of 950 square kilometres has sal and bamboo forests, meadows, grasslands and plateaus, nestled in the Banjar and Halon valleys of the Satpura ranges, to which are added an abundance of animals and birds. Three classics that feature Kanha are *The Highlands of Central India* by Forsyth, *Wild Animals in Central India* by A.A. Dunbar Brander and *The Deer and the Tiger* by George Schaller.

It is also the preferred destination for conservation experts all over the world. Stringent programmes of conservation of flora and fauna by dedicated forest officers have made it one of the best administered parks in Asia. The Kanha Tiger Reserve consists of the national park, which forms the core zone, surrounded by a buffer zone, bringing its total area to 945 square kilometres.

ABOVE

Spotted deer grazing in Kanha National Park.

The British began by protecting not birds and animals, but trees, for the commercial value of forest produce; but by the 1920s, they were forced to take cognisance of the sharp decline in wildlife, resulting from the clearing of forests for cultivation and timber, growth of the cattle population, and rampant poaching. Two sanctuaries were created, one in the Banjar Valley in 1933, and other in the Halon Valley in 1935.

These afforded reasonable protection till 1947, in which year privileged hunting permits were issued for tigers in the sanctuary, as a result of which, between then and 1951 some thirty tigers were shot. The government then sat up and took a series of measures: the reconstitution of the sanctuary in 1952, the creation of Kanha National Park in 1955, the halting of all forestry operations in 1959, and the constitution of Project Tiger in 1974.

Most people visit sanctuaries mainly to see the tiger. So it is with Kanha, but the difference is that on reaching the national park, the captivating sight of stately sal forests and the meadows, which retain a pristine appeal welcome a visitor; if there ever was a Garden of Eden, this is what it must have been like. Then there is the thrill of going to bed in a cot in the open, and waking up to find a herd of Chital around you, an experience many have had. Driving through the park is unforgettable, with sudden sights of hordes of Chital, an aristocratic Sambar with majestic headgear, surrounded by its harem, the handsome Barasingha, with antlers up to twelve points, (from where it derives its name), found only in Kanha, the massive, brooding Indian gaur (Bison), the world's largest buffalo, whom even the tiger would hesitate to confront, a pack of Dholes or Wild dogs loping across the meadows at dawn, large packs of whom have been known to kill tigers, scurrying Wild boar that have a deceptive appeal if one is not aware that each of these ferocious animals pack 500 lbs

LEFT

A sal forest grove in Kanha National Park.

ABOVE

Indian gaur (Bison), Kanha National Park.

RIGHT

A majestic tiger settles down for the day at Kanha Tiger Reserve.

of pure aggression, Chital and langurs combine to detect predators, one from a height and the other from ground level, with the langurs producing the explosive hack, the alarm call that alerts all. A rare sight is the porcupine, whose method of self-defence is to rush, tail-first, towards its attacker; the longer quills may be left embedded, causing serious injury, leading tigers and leopards to become man-eaters. Equally rare is the Sloth bear, a massive, lumbering beast, weighing 280 - 320 lbs, which can be sighted on the meadows, eating the fallen flowers of the mahua tree. Like the bear, the leopard is a nocturnal animal, and therefore also difficult to sight, but when spotted, is a delight to watch.

The highlight of a visit to any sanctuary is of course a sight of the tiger, normally seen at a safe distance, preferably from on top of an elephant. However its size, grace and beauty never cease to fascinate and create awe, which is perhaps, at its roots, atavistic.

Kanha also has birdlife which is both profuse and fascinating – the tally of species would probably exceed 200. Birds are normally seen in the mixed and bamboo forest of the hills, and at *nala*s near the meadows, the best times for sighting being early mornings and late afternoons. Birds at Kanha include Median egrets, Black ibises, Lesser whistling teals, kites, Crested serpent eagles, vultures, Red-wattled lapwings, pigeons, doves, parakeets, owls, White-breasted kingfishers, Grey hornbills, barbets, woodpeckers, swallows, drongos, Black-headed orioles and babblers.

If you are young, a visit to Kanha will be one of life's most precious memories, and if old, leave you with the feeling that you have been blessed with an insight of the glory of the Creator.

KHAJURAHO – BANDHAVGARH

Khajuraho | Once in a blue moon, once in several centuries, does something materialise, as delicate, intricate and sublime as the Khajuraho group of temples, which seems as something only the gods could have created. Appropriately therefore, as legend has it, one summer night, Hemvati, the exquisitely beautiful daughter of Hemraj, the royal priest of Varanasi was bathing in a lotus pool, when the Moon God himself, dazzled by her beauty, descended and ravished her. Later repenting, he blessed her with a son, Chandravarman, who was endowed with both strength and valour and who went on to found the Chandella dynasty. Equally appropriate is the fact that the Khajuraho group of temples, built by the Chandellas can be said to be a celebration of woman and her relationship with man.

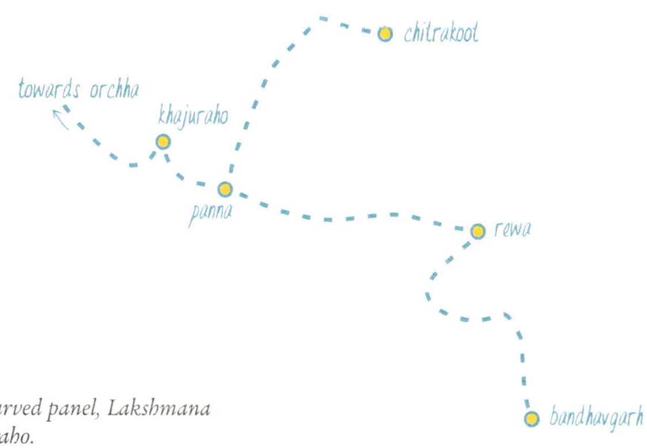

LEFT

A beautifully carved panel, Lakshmana Temple, Khajuraho.

The Chandellas grew, from being feudatories of the imperial Pratiharas, to rulers of one of the major kingdoms of the north, not hesitating to take on Mahmud of Ghazni and Muhammad of Ghur. Combining martial traits with a love for the arts, they built both impregnable fortresses, Kalinjar and Ajaygarh, and temples that were exquisite and magnificent. Of the eighty-five temples built, only twenty-five survive. What is inexplicable however, is, despite the fact that Khajuraho was for some time the capital of the Chandellas, there are no remains of any secular buildings.

After the end of the Chandella dynasty the temples remained lost and unknown till, centuries later, in 1838, T. S. Burt, Captain of the British Army travelling through the forests, was told by his *palkiwala* of the monuments, and went on to discover what is now a UNESCO inscribed World Heritage Site.

Khajuraho, because of inaccessibility did not develop as a tourist destination, being visited only by the more adventurous, till the Poddars, a business family, displaying commendable entrepreneurship, built a first class hotel, and persuaded the powers that be to have a Boeing land there. Today it is part of the 'Golden Triangle' – Agra-Khajuraho-Varanasi.

Government agencies fortunately were sensitive and imaginative enough to prepare a Master Plan for Khajuraho and organise the Khajuraho Festival of Dances there. The Master Plan ensured that the western group of temples had, just outside its periphery, a large paved plaza, providing an appropriate approach, instead of the filth and cesspools that normally greet one when visiting monuments, and that no building rose above to overshadow the *shikhara* of the Kandariya Mahadeva Temple.

In 1975, the Khajuraho Festival of Dances was the first major festival to be organised in a monument, where some of the country's finest artists performed against the magnificent backdrop of the Kandariya Mahadeva Temple. It was said that after a thousand years, the dancer returned to the temple, so that one had inspiration, and the other, life.

A visit to Khajuraho begins, and very often ends, with a round of the western group of temples, which is understandable, given the fact that this group contains the finest temples, sculpture and architecture, and what the eastern and southern groups have to offer are not significantly different. Going around the temples is strenuous, especially if it is hot, and the mind tends to wander since there are apparent repetitions; therefore if one has not visited Khajuraho several times earlier, or is not a scholar, and the duration of stay limited, it would make sense to focus on less, and imbibe more.

The temples are built of sandstone, light in colour, which add to the delicacy of the sculptures, especially when viewed during early mornings and late evenings. Most temples have common structural elements, irrespective of the deities to whom these are dedicated – Vishnu, Shiva, or a Jain *tirthankara*, and are built on raised platforms that provide both a setting to the structures and

an opportunity to circumambulate them. All temples have an *ardhamandapa* (entrance porch), a *mandapa* (hall), an *antarala* (vestibule), and a *garbha-griha* (sanctum), larger temples having a *maha-mandapa*, and an inner ambulatory. The forms of the temples possess something of the qualities of great music in them, individual roofs over halls rising and falling rhythmically, with a continuous vertical ascent, till, at the *shikhara* there is a soaring to a grand crescendo. These are the finest of specimens of temple architecture of Central India, reaching maturity in the Kandariya Mahadeva Temple.

ABOVE

Detail of a wall of sculptures at Jagadambi Temple, Khajuraho.

Splendid though the architecture may be, what draws people to Khajuraho are the sculptures, a profusion of which adorn the outer walls of the temples, which include formal cult images, gods and goddesses, attendants, *apsara*s and *sura sundaris*, depicting scenes of what happens all around one – people hunting, teaching, praying, playing musical instruments, making love and war. The sculptures seem not to be chiseled, but mobile, liquid, poured into perfect moulds, representing the creations of people who exult in the joy of living, with all its fascinating variety, and the ethereal quality of the love between man and woman. Which brings us to the subject of eroticism.

Much has been written about what is considered erotic in the sculptures of Khajuraho, and there have been various theories about its origins. Many have felt that it was a reflection of the depths of depravity to which society in those times had sunk, others that it displays the liberal attitude Indians had towards sex, as is the case in the *Kamasutra*, still others that it depicts the practises of some medieval sects.

It is necessary here to ask ourselves whether depictions of nudity or the variety of physical relationships between men and women are ipso facto erotic or obscene. The answer would be an obvious 'no', because if this was so, great art all over the world, especially the extraordinary creations of the Renaissance masters, would suffer from pejorative connotations.

The dictionary definition of 'erotic' is, what 'arouses sexual desire or excitement'; therefore only that which has the primary intention of arousing sexual desire, or what is offending to the senses should be considered erotic. It can, on the contrary, be argued that the sculptures of Khajuraho represent the finest depictions of the human body, especially of the female form, and that these are a toast to, and celebration of woman, the human form, and love in all its glorious variety, in states of abandon. These are in fact a visual feast, and the ultimate test is, that while viewing these, nudity is not even noticed.

It has also to be remembered that the sculptures of Khajuraho are the creations of people who regarded *kama*, or the pursuit of pleasure, as one of the means of approaching the transcendent, and that for them the human act of making love reflected the divine act of creation. If some sculptures depict the unnatural, this is only part of the reflection of reality as a whole. On the whole, visiting the temples of Khajuraho is an uplifting experience.

One can begin a tour of the temples at the Varaha Temple. The striking image of the boar incarnation of Vishnu is of sandstone that remains highly polished, with 674 images of gods and goddesses that from a distance, combine to look like a coat of armour. Varaha stands over a fluid *Seshanaga* (serpent) and the feet of the broken image of the Earth Goddess whom Varaha rescued from the waters.

In front of this shrine is the Lakshmana Temple, the earliest of Khajuraho's major temples. Constructed by Yashovarman in the middle of the tenth century, it has Vaikuntha, an image of Vishnu as its main idol, with three heads and four arms, the central one being human, flanked by those of a boar and a lion. Apart from domestic scenes, sculptures include panels of hunting and battle, glimpses of the life of Krishna, and the incarnations of Vishnu. This well preserved structure possesses all the major architectural elements of the developed temples of this period, but what is striking is the *makara torana*, an arch at the entrance, produced from what flows out of the gaping mouths of crocodiles on either side.

The Vishvanatha Temple, built at the start of the eleventh century, in architectural style, falls between the Lakshmana and the Kandariya Mahadeva temples. Like the Lakshmana Temple it has all the elements of the developed Khajuraho temple – the entrance, *mandapa*, *maha-mandapa* and the *garbha-griha*. It is a *panchayatana* temple (a five-shrined structure), with subsidiary shrines at four corners and has some of the finest sculptures in the group. The temple is dedicated to Shiva Markatesvara, and an inscription states that there were two *linga*s, one of emerald and one of stone, of which only the stone one survives.

What is interesting about the Jagadambi Temple is that though it has the image of Parvati in the sanctum, it was originally dedicated to Vishnu, which is evidenced by the fact that there is a figure of the deity on the doorway of the sanctum. Thus, figures on the entrance to a *garbha-griha* enable identification of the main deity of a temple, even if it is removed or destroyed. This temple also has some very fine renderings of gods and goddesses, including one of Yama, the Lord of Death.

Contiguous with the Jagadambi Temple is the Kandariya Mahadeva Temple, the most magnificent of all the temples of Khajuraho and one of the finest creations of Indian architecture. The temple contains the usual architectural features, but on a scale that is grand, with superb proportions.

Two other features are spectacular, the first being the variety and quality of sculptures. Apart from amorous couples there are sculptures of gods and goddesses, *apsara*s, *mithuna*s and *sura sundari*s, dancers, devotees, acrobats, musicians, processions of warriors, hunters, elephants and horses. The quality of carvings is superb, and though perfectly proportioned, are elongated, something which endows them with added grace and elegance. The second is the manner in which the eighty-four small replicas of the *shikhara*, ascend and embellish the grand *shikhara*, that soars to the sky, lofty and monumental. The temple is truly a song in stone, on an epic scale.

Though in no way competing with the Kandariya Mahadeva Temple, three temples deserve to be visited. The first is the Chitragupta Temple, the only one at Khajuraho dedicated to Surya, the Sun God, the figure wearing boots stands in a chariot with

seven horses. Sculptures include elephant fights, hunting scenes, dancing girls, stone carriers, and divine couples like Brahma-Brahmani, Shiva-Parvati, Lakshmi-Narayana, and Bhairava-Bhairavi and an eleven-headed Vishnu.

The second is the Matangeshvara Temple, the only temple at Khajuraho in which worship still takes place. It is one of the earliest, and though devoid of embellishments, has a massive *linga*, worshipped by thousands of devotees visiting it during Maha Shivaratri.

Also different is the Chausath-Yogini Temple, the earliest temple in Khajuraho, and perhaps the earliest *yogini* shrine in India, dedicated to the sixty-four aspects of the Mother Goddess. Other temples in the western group are dedicated to Shiva and Parvati, and the Lalguan-Mahadeva Temple.

The eastern group of temples seems somewhat dull in comparison with the western group, but is of interest to scholars of temple sculptures and architecture, since the temples represent stages in development. There are many interesting aspects of these temples. The Brahma Temple is in fact dedicated to Vishnu, but carries the name of Brahma due to the four faced *linga* in the sanctum. There is a temple devoted to Vamana, which is a *nirandhara* structure – one without an ambulatory.

The Javari Temple, though a *nirandhara* structure, is a fine piece of architecture, well proportioned, with a soaring *shikhara*, well-carved *makara torana* and sculptures.

There is a group of Jain temples in the complex; the Ghantai, Adinatha, Parsvanatha and Shantinatha. The Ghantai Temple gets its local name from the bell motifs on its pillars. Though twice the size of the Parsvanatha Temple, all that remains are the entrance porch and *maha mandapa*.

What is interesting about Parsvanatha Temple is that despite the fact that it is a Jain temple, dedicated to the first *tirthankara*, it has Vaishnava statues of Parasurama, Balarama, Rama, Sita, Hanuman as well as images of Agni, Shiva, Kama and Lakshmi-Narayana. The *sura sundari* figures are also amongst the finest in Khajuraho.

The southern group has only two temples; the Duladeo and Chaturbhuja.

LEFT

Light and sound show, Khajuraho.

Architecturally, the Duladeo Temple has something in common with southern temples. Its sculptures with excessive ornamentation lack movement, grace and vitality as well as depict the exhaustion of talent by the twelfth century.

The Chaturbhuja Temple is the only one without amorous couples, and the quality of sculptures is mediocre. There is however one exceptional piece, a four-armed Vishnu, with an expression of great bliss and serenity.

While leaving Khajuraho one cannot but pause to wonder how the Chandellas, known for their valour and martial prowess had the inclination and time to build so many temples that represent an outpouring of the finest creative skills that man is capable of. This is perhaps explained by the fact that Indian kings and emperors were often enigmatic, like Siddhartha, who, at the peak of his power, renounced the world, or Emperor Ashoka who abandoned war after conquest. It is such enigmas that have given Indian civilisation a quality that is unique.

Khajuraho has, apart from the Bandhavgarh National Park, a number of places nearby, which are in their own ways, very interesting. To begin with there are two forts of the Chandellas, Kalinjar and Ajaygarh.

Ajaygarh was the capital of Chandellas for some time. It is situated on a plateau, so it is a difficult climb to reach there, but this is amply rewarded by the wonderful view from it. In the fort are remains of palaces, temples and tanks.

Kalinjar, also built by Chandellas, situated on rocky terrain, had a reputation for invincibility. Attacked by Afghan invaders and Mahmud of Ghazni, it fell finally to Emperor Akbar, who gifted it to Birbal, from whom it passed to Raja Chhatrasal.

Raja Chhatrasal, was one of the three rulers to rise against Aurangzeb, the others being Shivaji and Guru Gobind Singh. He made Panna, twenty-five kilometres from Khajuraho, his capital. Panna is famous for its diamond mine, national park, (declared a reserve under Project Tiger in 1995) and the Ken Gharial Sanctuary.

A complete contrast to the forts and places associated with the brave, are the three other places close to Khajuraho, well worth visiting.

Chitrakoot, where Rama, Sita and Lakshmana spent eleven of their fourteen years of exile, has an atmosphere of total tranquility, with its combination of forests, streams and rivers.

Abdur Rahim Khan-e-Khanan, Akbar's prime minister, and a poet, used to visit Chitrakoot whenever depression overtook him. The town has many places associated with *Ramayana*, saints and miracles. It is believed that Brahma had performed penance at the Matha Gajendranath Shiv Temple; Param Kutir is the place where Lakshmana was supposed to have built a hut for the three exiles;

RIGHT

Vishvanatha Temple, in the western part of Khajuraho.

ABOVE

Sharada Mata Temple, Maihar.

RIGHT

Chitrakoot, famous for its association with the Ramayana *is also known for its Diwali celebrations.*

Bharata was supposed to have met Rama at a place where the Bharat Milap Temple stands; Sita is supposed to have bathed in Janaki Kund; Sati Anasuya Ashram was visited by Rama, Sita and Lakshmana; and Kamadgiri is the hill that fulfills all desires. This is gentle Hinduism at its finest.

Another place close to Khajuraho that has an association with Rama, is Ramvan, which houses a single man's collection, of what is perhaps the largest number of handwritten manuscripts associated with the *Ramayana* in the country.

Also exuding peace and tranquility is Maihar, where one of the greatest masters of Hindustani classical music, Ustad Allauddin Khan established a college for music. And what a stream of great artistes it produced; Pandit Ravi Shankar, Pannalal Ghosh, Pandit Hariprasad Chaurasia, Ustad Ali Akbar Khan, and Pandit Vishwamohan Bhatt. Maihar has nurtured the famous Maihar Band and is venue for the annual Allaudin Khan Sangeet Samaroh, one of the finest music festivals in the country.

Apart from connoisseurs and lovers of Indian classical music Maihar with its sacred shrine of Sharada Mata, attracts a large number of pilgrims as well. The hill of Maihar is truly a town where culture abundantly overflows.

Bandhavgarh | After Khajuraho, apart from visiting nearby places of interest mentioned above; the forts, Panna, Ramvan and Maihar, it would be well worth your while to drive to Bandhavgarh National Park, a little over 200 kilometres away, spending at least a night and a day there. In the jargon of tourist operators, this is the 'temple-tiger tour'. When compared to Kanha, the park is small, 449 square kilometres. It is, however, this compactness that results in almost all visitors to Bandhavgarh being rewarded by the excitement of the sight of a tiger.

Apart from this important advantage, Bandhavgarh also has the

added attractions of undulating terrain, and a picturesque medieval fort on a hill, which incidentally was also inhabited by the Chandella dynasty. The fort was later occupied by the Baghels, from whom the Maharajahs of Rewa trace their ancestry. Bandhavgarh was a hunting ground for them.

The associations of the fort go back to *Ramayana* – it is believed that Rama, after defeating Ravana, stopped here, gifting the fort, built by Hanuman's associates, to his brother Lakshmana, who is worshipped here. On the way to the fort is a statue of a reclining Vishnu, close to the feet of which flows a stream, therefore named Charanganga.

In 1951, a White tiger cub was discovered around Bandhavgarh, which vets confirmed was not an albino, but the result of a very unusual recessive gene surfacing. From this tiger, named Mohan, came other White tigers, now a major attraction in

ABOVE

The magnificent beast caught up close, hiding in foliage at Bandhavgarh Tiger Reserve.

RIGHT

The statue of a reclining Vishnu on the way to the Bandhavgarh Fort.

zoos scattered all over the world. But there was a time when tigers were more shot at than admired. To shoot 109 tigers was considered a good omen for a Maharajah of Rewa, and when Maharajah Venkat Raman Singh shot 111 tigers by 1914, it was an occasion for great celebration; Gulab Singh of Rewa was credited with having shot 480!

However, one should refrain from being judgmental, whatever be the inclination to do so, because it must be remembered that those were very different times, when duels, battles and *shikar* were considered macho, something all young men were brought up to indulge in.

Bandhavgarh has been and will be a destination for tourists who want to see the tiger. However, like Kanha, there is much to see apart from the tiger. To begin with, it is a sylvan paradise, Nature at its purest, which like the tiger touches an atavistic chord in most of us. If Kanha has its rolling, flowing meadows, Bandhavgarh in early winter, is a carnival of colours, birds, blooms and butterflies.

Again, like Kanha, it has other animals apart from the tiger, which are a delight to watch, some awesome, others lithe and graceful, expressing in their movements the joy of life, and birds who embellish the scene with flights of abandon, and songs sung for the joy of singing alone. If anything approaches what might have been the Garden of Eden, it is national parks such as Kanha and Bandhavgarh. The vegetation is mainly of sal forest in the valleys and on the lower slopes gradually changing to mixed deciduous forest on the hills and in the hotter, drier areas of the park in the south and west. Bamboo is found all over the park. Grassy meadows are spread over 6 per cent of the area.

Bandhavgarh's wildlife is typical of the forests of Central India, with certain species such as the Nilgai and the Chinkara which are typical of drier, more open country. There are over twenty species of large mammals, the most commonly found being; the Common langur, Wild pig, Chital, Sambar, Muntjac or Barking deer and Chausingha. Also seen are the Indian hare, Indian porcupine, jackal, fox, Sloth bear, mongoose, hyena, leopard, apart from, of course, the tiger.

The park also has many species of birds, which are seen throughout the area, but mostly along streams and clearings. Migratory birds visit it in winter. Commoner species include egrets, Pond herons, Black ibises, Lesser whistling teals, Crested serpent eagles, vultures, Red-wattled lapwings, Green sandpipers, pigeons, doves, parakeets, kingfishers, hornbills, woodpeckers, swallows, drongos, minivets, babblers and flycatchers.

Though Bandhavgarh may lack the spread and drama of some of the other national parks, it remains a gem of a park, in which one is almost certain to meet up with the majestic animal that people all over the world most yearn to see – the magnificent tiger.

INDORE - MANDU - OMKARESHWAR - MAHESHWAR - UJJAIN

Indore | Indore is a convenient base to visit Mandu, Omkareshwar, Maheshwar, Ujjain and other places in this fascinating region of Malwa; located on the Agra-Mumbai road, it also has good air and rail connections.

Like Gwalior, Indore was also a city founded by Maratha chieftains. The accomplishments of Marathas of the eighteenth century were nothing short of amazing – conquests of enormous territories with minimal resources.

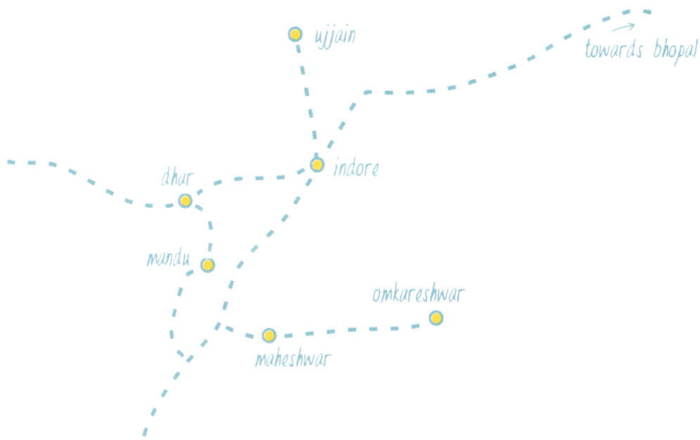

LEFT

The opulent interiors of the Darbar Hall, Lalbagh Palace, Indore.

ABOVE

Subedar Malhar Rao Holkar I, the founder of the Holkar dynasty.

RIGHT

The Old Rajwada Palace in the heart of town, Indore.

The founder of the Holkar dynasty, Malhar Rao Holkar came from humble stock, being a shepherd from a village named Hol, but apart from tending animals, was a born warrior and a natural leader of men. The Peshwa at Pune was impressed by what he saw and appointed him to command the Maratha forces in Malwa. Malhar Rao was unusual not only in what he was personally endowed with, but equally in the manner in which he was able to spot Ahilyabai, and groom her to be one of the nation's greatest rulers.

The Holkars founded and nurtured Indore, and much of what they left has survived, the most significant being the two palaces; the Rajwada and the Lalbagh.

The Rajwada Palace, situated in the centre of town was reduced to a facade after the fire in 1984. It is a seven-storied building, with a large courtyard within, surrounded by galleries. The structure is imposing but not architecturally significant.

The Lalbagh Palace, on the other hand, has great elegance. A magnificent gateway, being the replica of the main gate of Buckingham Palace, but twice as large, opens onto a very impressive driveway, leading to the palace. Most of the furniture and ornamentation within is of the late Regency and early Georgian styles. The palace has Italian marble columns, chandeliers, Persian carpets, Belgium stained-glass windows, Italian style wall paintings, a wooden ballroom floor mounted on springs and stuffed animals.

Also worth a visit is the Residency, an imposing colonial structure with an impressive approach; those climbing the many steps leading to the building are bound to be in awe of the presence inside.

Close to the Residency is the Central Museum, which has a unique collection of fine medieval stone sculptures from Hinglajgarh. An enterprising curator visited the site at Hinglajgarh on the border of

Madhya Pradesh and Rajasthan, and after taking permission from his senior officers returned with twelve truckloads of sculptures in a perfect state of preservation, to form the richest collection of medieval sculptures from a single site in the country. Hardly any exhibition of Indian art abroad fails to display an exhibit or two from the Hinglajgarh collection of this museum. Apart from the sculpture collection, there is a Coin Gallery which has a large number of rare coins gifted by personal collectors of Indore.

Contrasting with the Lalbagh Palace and the Residency is Kanch Mandir, a Jain temple made entirely of glass, built by a wealthy merchant in the early twentieth century. Also worth a visit are the royal *chhatris*, the cenotaphs of the Holkars.

Gwalior and Indore were both creations of rulers who came from the same part of the country, so it is strange that Gwalior remains a somewhat crude and provincial city and Indore is a throbbing, thriving, commercial city, often compared to Mumbai.

This is probably the legacy of the liberal rule of Rani Ahilyabai, who will be looked at in more detail a little later.

Mandu | Two medieval introductions to the flavour of Mandu. Ahmad-Ul-Umri Turkoman in 1599, in his poetic account of the tale of Rupmati and Baz Bahadur writes of Mandu:

> For them who know not Malwa nor yet Mandu, be it here set down that Malwa lieth in the central parts of the country of Hindustan, lifted high upon a tableland behind the Vindhya mountains. Therein is neither exceeding heat nor exceeding cold, and the nights of land of Malwa, are they not famous from ancient days? Even as men say, 'The dawn of Banaras, the evening of Oudh, the night of Malwa.' Within the land of Malwa, lieth Mandu, the great fortress, jutting out like bastion from the tableland in the valley of Rewa, the river which men of these times call Narbada.

Emperor Jahangir wrote:

> What words of mine can describe the beauty of the grass and the wild flowers? They clothe each hill and dale, each slope and plain. I know of no place so pleasant in climate and so pretty in scenery as Mandu in the rainy season. This month of July, which is one of the most famous months

RIGHT

The tomb of Hoshang Shah in Mandu, situated next to the Jami Masjid, is made entirely of marble.

> of the hot season, the sun being in Leo, one cannot sleep within the house without a coverlet, and during the day there is no need for a fan.

Let Jahangir introduce us to the monuments as well:

> On Monday the 23 Ispandad, the last month of the Persian year, when the last quarter of the day had passed, I mounted my elephant, and, in good fortune, and under kindly influences, made my happy entry into the Fort of Mandu...During my passage across the hill top I scattered rupees 1,500. Before my arrival, Abdul Karim, the Engineer, had been sent by me to repair the buildings...On the whole, he had provided quarters for me, the like of which have probably never been built in any other place... I wish it had been possible to construct buildings like these in all cities likely to be visited by royalty.

Ninety-eight kilometres from Indore lies the fortress city of Mandu. As you drive up to plateaux, the remains of towers, mosques and tombs flash past, heralding the approach to the city. Staying in Mandu is not merely a visit to monuments, but a unique experience of living in the medieval ages, embellished by the legendary love story of Rupmati and Baz Bahadur.

The road winds up and the massive fortifications suddenly loom over you — strong and sure. There are a series of gates, with impressive names; Delhi, Alamgir and Bhangi Darwaza. Surrounded by a perimeter wall of forty-five kilometres, the defence arrangements were, according to the chronicler Firishta to be, "the most extraordinary in the then world."

Past these you enter a plateau of 12,000 acres, six to eight kilometres in length and five to six kilometres in breadth with fields, gardens, wells, lakes and ponds, bazaars, roads, dwellings, rest-houses, baths, mosques and palaces.

Mandu is to be visited after the rains and entered at dusk. Come well read and spend a few days here — legend, greenery, lakes, ruins and magnificent views of the plains below will enchant you.

Mandu dates back to the sixth century AD, a hill fort under the name Mandapa Durga, whose Prakrit equivalent is Mandava. Malwa grew to be an independent kingdom by the end of the tenth century under the Paramaras, with the capital at Ujjain and later Dhar, with two great kings; Munja and Raja Bhoja.

In 1305 a general of Alauddin Khalji attacked Mandu, slew the ruler and Malwa was made a

LEFT

A kund *(bathing place) on the terrace of Jahaz Mahal, Mandu.*

ABOVE

Hindola Mahal, Mandu.

RIGHT

The spectacular "stone ship palace", Jahaz Mahal, Mandu.

part of the Delhi Sultanate. Governors held their capital at Dhar and occasionally camped at Mandu. Dilawar Khan Ghuri, governor at the time of Muhammad-bin-Tughlaq declared independence in 1401. He kept his capital at Dhar but made visits to Mandu as well. After his death in 1405, fortifications were undertaken by his son who ascended the throne assuming the regal name of Hoshang Shah in 1405, and shifted his capital to Mandu.

Hoshang Shah was a great warrior and there were conflicts with Delhi, Jaunpur and Gujarat, but he also found time to build and leave behind splendid edifices like the Jami Masjid, the Delhi Gate and his own tomb, which are certainly amongst the finest architectural specimens of those times. The fortifications were stupendous for an age when gun powder and cannon were unknown. Most important of all, he was loved by his people.

Work on the Jami Masjid, designed after the great Mosque of Damascus, was commenced by Hoshang Shah and the building was completed by Mahmud Khilji in 1454; a structure of massive proportions and stern simplicity. The prayer hall has numerous rows of arches and pillars with fifty-eight small domes and three large ones, the pulpit raised, with an elegant marble dome, and a high platform, resembling a throne. Its acoustics are amazing, a whisper uttered at one end being clearly audible at the other. The Masjid reflects the piety and strength of the great ruler.

Hoshang Shah's tomb is supposed to be one of the finest monuments of the East. It acquired sanctity and till the nineteenth century, Urs (the largest Muslim fair in India) used to be held here every year. An inscription records that four architects of Shah Jahan visited the tomb in 1659 AD to pay a homage to the builders, one of them being Ustad Hamid, who was closely associated with the construction of Taj Mahal.

Hoshang Shah was succeeded by Muhammad Shah in 1435, who was poisoned a year later, bringing an end to the Ghuri dynasty.

Mahmud Shah, the Khilji Sultan, a great warrior under whom Malwa reached its widest extent, waged wars against the rulers of Jaunpur, Gujarat and the Deccan. A seven storied structure was raised to commemorate a victory over the Rana of Mewar.

Besides being a warrior he was a patron of learning and left behind a madrasa known as Ashrafi Mahal, with a large impressive courtyard, with cells all around, to face the Jami Masjid. His buildings though lofty in conception, were constructed without care and expertise, leading to their eventual collapse.

A very unusual ruler was Ghiyas-ud-din Khilji (1469 - 1500) who devoted his career to peaceful pursuits. Though he never touched wine, his sexual appetite was enormous, the number of women in his harem being an unbelievable 15,000, in addition to which he had 500 Turkish and 500 Abyssinian women guards! Ghiyas-ud-din left behind the Jahaz and Hindola Mahals.

Mandu was also known as Shadiabad, city of joy, a whole city crafted for pleasure. If there is one structure that epitomises this pursuit it is Jahaz Mahal, a superb palace that lends itself most naturally for ceremonies. Like all significant structures in Mandu, the combination of size, severity, and lack of ornamentation, gives it a grandeur that inspires awe, to which is added the intermingling of water and stone — lakes on either side, or pools within. With a spectacular terrace and windows lit up during ceremonies, from far it must have resembled an enormous ship.

Nur Jahan resided in this palace, and Jahangir wrote about one of the many magnificent ceremonies that took place here:

> It was a wonderful assembly. In the beginning of the evening they lighted lanterns and lamps all round the tanks and buildings and lighting up was carried out, the like of which has perhaps never been arranged in any place. The lanterns and the lamps cast their reflection on the water and it appeared as if the whole surface of the tank was a plain of fire. A grand entertainment took place and the drunkards indulged themselves to excess.

The second palace built by Ghiyas-ud-din was the Hindola Mahal, which literally means, swinging palace due to its sloping walls, which resemble the sides of a gigantic swing. The exterior of the structure, like others in Mandu, has a simplicity that adds dignity, but does not detract from majesty. However, what is interesting and more romantic is what exists inside. On both sides of the hall there are six arched openings above which are windows filled with beautiful *jali* (tracery) work for admitting light and air. The flight of sloping stages was meant for royal ladies to go up in palanquins on horses or elephants. The subterranean chambers are cool, and it is said that this is where the ladies resided. When taken down, one is often greeted by flights of hundreds of bats, which one imaginative guide described as the souls of the departed queens and princesses.

Ghiyas-ud-din's rule was marked by order, liberality, justice and charity, but it ended with him being poisoned by his son Nasir-ud-din. As poetic justice, Nasir-ud-din's reign of an unhappy ten years was spent mostly in dealing with feuds within the kingdom.

In 1526, Bahadur Shah of Gujarat invaded Malwa and annexed the territory, which remained with Gujarat till 1534, when it was conquered by Humayun.

As soon as Humayun left Malwa, Mallu Khan, an officer of the former Khilji dynasty reconquered territories, assuming the title of Quadir Shah.

In 1542 Sher Shah conquered Malwa and appointed Shujaat Khan as the governor, who died in 1554. One of his sons Malik Bayazid crowned himself 'Baz Bahadur' who ruled from 1554 to 1561.

If Mandu, with its lakes, palaces and tombs, is a rare treasure of India, the tale of the romance and love of Rupmati and Baz Bahadur is its most precious gem, whose most exquisite rendering is by Ahmad-ul-Umri Turkoman, in 1599, translated and introduced by L.M.Crump.

Baz Bahadur slew one brother Daulat Khan by treachery, and defeated other

ABOVE

A painting of Rupmati and Baz Bahadur of Mandu, legendary for their love story.

brother, Mustafa Khan in battle. However soon thereafter he himself suffered a humiliating defeat at the hands of the Gond Queen, Rani Durgavati. He then abandoned arms totally, and devoted himself to love and song. It was said that in his court the voice of music was never silent.

As per the folklore, once while hunting in the valley by the River Rewa, he came upon Rupmati, the exquisitely beautiful daughter of a local Rajput nobleman, singing and bathing in a pool with her friends, and was intoxicated by her beauty and voice. Rupmati's father opposed the alliance, but Baz Bahadur came the next day and carried a not unwilling Rupmati away!

Bright and happy were the days that followed for Rupmati, who bathed in the pools of Jahaz Mahal, or spent long days by the cool waters of the Champa Baoli. On Baz Bahadur's return they would sing to each other, songs of love which they composed, spending evening after evening on the roof of Jahaz Mahal.

One day when wandering on the parapets Rupmati spied her beloved River Rewa, like a stretch of silver, in the valley below. Baz Bahadur thereafter constructed two *chhatri*s popularly known as Rupmati's pavilion, and she spent many happy hours on its splendid terrace with its magnificent view of the valley and the river, and when evening set, the couple often sang there together. This was too beautiful to last, and in 1561 the imperial forces of the Mughals under Adham Khan, attacked and defeated Baz Bahadur in battle. Adham Khan hearing of the great beauty of Rupmati was determined to possess her, and sent a message of his coming to take her. Let Ahmad-ul-Umri Turkoman describe what happened thereafter.

> That very night that Adham Khan celebrated his feast, he caused the royal palace to be garnished for the new king of love. Rupmati, having finished her bathing, gave order for her body to be adorned with the very bridal dress that Baz Bahadur had given her. After this was done, she took her *been* in her hand and sang songs to melt the heart...until she was beside herself. Then retiring to her bed-chamber she took poison of powdered diamond.

But the legend of Rupmati and Baz Bahadur and their love lives on, as do the songs they sung.

> Seek not on earth my grave when life depart my sepulcher is every faithful heart. Lady fear not the sorrows of this world. Thy trials are over. The song of thy faithfulness will warm the hearts of men till doomsday, and on the story of thy end, the eyes of all lovers will ever drop a tribute of tears.

The memories of Nur Jahan and Jahangir, and of Rupmati and Baz Bahadur do not haunt the ruins of Mandu but instead imbue these with life, making Mandu, with its lakes, palaces, forests and memories, truly one of the most romantic places in the world.

Omkareshwar | After visiting Mandu it is suggested that the return journey to Indore should not be via Dhar, but Maheshwar and Omkareshwar. Omkareshwar, idyllically situated on the River Narmada, is said to derive its name from the fact that two hills and the valley in between resemble the syllable *Om*. The quaint picturesque town has one of the twelve *jyotirlinga*s, the other eleven being located at Somnath and Nageshwar in Gujarat, Mallikarjuna in Andhra Pradesh, Mahakaleshwar in Madhya Pradesh, Kedarnath in Uttarakhand, Bhimashankar, Trayambakeshwar, Ghrishneshwar in Maharashtra, Kashi Viswanath in Uttar Pradesh, Vaidyanatha in Bihar and Rameshwar in Tamil Nadu.

ABOVE

Shri Omkar Mandhata Temple, Omkareshwar.

The *jyotirlinga*s are so named because Shiva was supposed to have revealed himself in the form of *jyoti* (light). If only psychologically, the combination of light and the *linga* appear empowering.

The principal shrine at Omkareshwar is Shri Omkar Mandhata Temple, constructed by the Paramaras in the eleventh century, and rebuilt by the Holkars in the nineteenth century, which houses one of the twelve *jyotirlinga*s. It is therefore the main attraction for multitudes of pilgrims from all over the country.

There are many other places of pilgrimage on this island which include the Mamleshwar Temple on the other side of the river, Ashapuri Temple, Gauri Somnath Temple, Siddhanath Temple and Govindeshwar Gufa, is the place where Adi Shankaracharya was said to have received *diksha* from Guru Gobind Bhagwapat.

Maheshwar | As mentioned earlier, while driving back from Mandu to Indore, a fascinating detour is to go via Omkareshwar and Maheshwar. Like Omkareshwar, this city is also situated on the banks of the Narmada. Maheshwar is a very picturesque sight, especially when viewed from the river itself.

Before describing Maheshwar, it would be worthwhile to pause and reflect on the Narmada. The river is known as *sarvatra punya,* that is, unlike other sacred rivers, which acquire sanctity at specific places, the Narmada is regarded as being sacred everywhere. It is said to be the lifeline of Madhya Pradesh emerging from Amarkantak, descending to the Marble Rocks at Jabalpur, flowing broad-bossomed at Hoshangabad and then past Omkareshwar and Maheshwar.

Author-administrator Ashok Vajpeyi has this to say about the Narmada:

> In the unfathomable depth of its waters Narmada reflects the plurality, the multiplicity, the richness and the dynamism of Madhya Pradesh; its earthiness, its rockiness, its deep-rooted mysteries and its ceaseless flow. Narmada is variously celebrated in romance and legend, in myths and memories, in verse and songs, in prayers and praise, in music, dance and sculpture, in literature and poetry.

Maheshwar was the capital of Rani Ahilyabai Holkar, a ruler compared to European rulers, Catherine the Great and Queen Elizabeth.

RIGHT

Temples in Maheshwar are known for their intricately carved overhanging balconies and splendid doorways.

ABOVE

Rani Ahilyabai Holkar, legendary ruler of Maheshwar.

Born in 1725 in a small village in Maharashtra, she was noticed by a commander of the Peshwas, Malhar Rao Holkar, who after observing her in a temple, and recognising her piety and character, brought her home, and prepared her as a bride for his son, Khande Rao. Khande Rao Holkar was killed in a battle in 1754. Twelve years later, when her father-in-law, Malhar Rao died, Ahilyabai Holkar petitioned the Peshwa to permit her to assume control of the administration. It is said that Malhar Rao trained her both in administration and war. She led her armies in battle and was most popular with her men. Aware of her remarkable attributes, the Peshwa granted permission.

Ahilyabai never observed purdah and met her subjects daily. At Maheshwar she built temples, ghats and developed the town as a centre of literature and music; she also encouraged the handloom industry from which emerged the famed Maheshwari saris. These saris are woven with distinctive designs involving stripes, checks and floral borders.

Jawaharlal Nehru wrote of Ahilyabai:

> The reign of Ahilyabai of Indore in Central India lasted for thirty years. This has become almost legendary as a period during which perfect order and good government prevailed and the people prospered. She was a very able ruler and organiser, highly respected during her lifetime, and considered as a saint by a grateful people after her death.

Dr Annie Besant had this to say of her:

> This great ruler in Indore encouraged all within her realm to do their best. Merchants produced their finest cloth, trade flourished, the farmers were at peace and oppression ceased, for

> each case that came to the Queen's notice was dealt with severely. She loved to see her people prosper, and to watch the fine cities grow, and to watch that her subjects were not afraid to display their wealth, lest the ruler should snatch it from them. Far and wide the roads were planted with shady trees, and wells were made, and rest-houses for travellers. The poor, the homeless, the orphaned were all helped according to their needs...Hindu and Musalman alike revered the famous Queen and prayed for her long life.

Apart from what she did within her kingdom, Rani Ahilyabai's extraordinary energy and piety can be witnessed by the fact that she built temples all over India including Amarkantak in Madhya Pradesh; Ayodhya and Varanasi in Uttar Pradesh; Dwarka in Gujarat; Kedarnath, Haridwar, Rishikesh in Uttarakhand; Jagannath Puri in Orissa; Kurukshetra in Haryana and Rameshwar in Tamil Nadu.

There is no doubt that, with her abilities, piety, courage and compassion for her people, Ahilyabai is one of the greatest rulers that India has known.

Apart from the temples and the ghats, what is worth seeing in Maheshwar is the palace. The Rajwada Palace built in 1776, houses an archaeological museum, the Rajgadi of Rani Ahilyabai from where she dispensed justice, and her private temple with her golden swing and silver Shiva idols. The palace is simple, but with the throne and temple it seems to embody her spirit. There is a panoramic view of the Narmada from the palace, but equally stunning is the view of the palace and the ghats from the river. Truly, a visit to Maheshwar is one that is both consoling and inspiring.

Ujjain

> It is remarkable how durable has been the position of Ujjayini, the capital of several Hindu dynasties in India, as the reference location for many of the Indian calendars. The Vikram Samvat calendar (with a zero point in 57 BC) apparently originated in this ancient capital city. It is also the base of the Saka system (zero point in 78 AD). Indeed even today, Ujjain's location is used to fix the anchor point of the Indian clock (serving, in this respect, as the Indian Greenwich). The Indian Standard Time that governs our lives still remains a close approximation of Ujjayini time – five hours and thirty minutes ahead of GMT.
>
> – Amartya Sen
> 'India through its Calendars'
> in the *Little Magazine*, Vol.1, No.1

Merely an hour's drive from Indore, is Ujjain, one of India's oldest cities, going back to the days of the Mahabharata. Known as Ujjayini it

ABOVE

An idol of Harsiddhi Ma (another name for Parvati) at Harsiddhi Temple, Ujjain.

RIGHT

Mahakaleshwara Temple, Ujjain.

was the capital of the kingdom of Avanti. Located here is Sandipani Ashram, the place where Sri Krishna along with Balrama and Sudama received education from Maharishi Sandipani.

Emperor Ashoka was the viceroy at Ujjain before he ascended the imperial throne, and it was from here that his son Mahendra and daughter Sanghamitra commenced their missionary journey to carry the message of Buddha right up to Sri Lanka.

After Ashoka, Ujjain had another remarkable ruler, Chandragupta Vikramaditya, whose court had the fabled *navaratna*s (nine jewels) including Kalidasa, who in his immortal poem *Mehgadootam* describes the passage of the cloud over Ujjayini.

In the sixth and seventh centuries Ujjain became a major centre of mathematical and astronomical research, producing luminaries like Brahmagupta and Varahamihira, and the Vikram Samvat calendar. Even today it remains an extremely important location for astrological predictions.

There are not many secular monuments left at Ujjain; a building worth visiting is the Kaliyadeh Palace, situated on the banks of River Shipra, built by Sultan Mahmud Khilji, the central dome of which is a beautiful example of Persian architecture. Two Persian inscriptions record the visits of Emperor Akbar and Jahangir.

From the ninth to twelfth century, Ujjain was ruled by the Paramaras. When Baz Bahadur of Mandu was defeated by Akbar, the city came under the Mughals. In the first half of eighteenth century Sawai Jai Singh was made governor of Malwa. With his interest in astronomy, he built an observatory similar to the ones at Jaipur, Delhi, Varanasi and Mathura. Remarkable as the rulers of Ujjain were, and splendid though their courts and palaces may have been, Ujjain's importance today stems mainly from it being one of the

श्री ओंकारेश्वर
महादेव मंदिर

most sacred cities for Hindus. The Simhastha Mela, the biggest Hindu fair, is held in Ujjain once in twelve years.

Ujjain is a temple town with many interesting shrines, the most important being the Mahakaleshwara Temple that houses one of the twelve *jyotirlinga*s. The *shivlinga* in this temple is guarded by a hooded silver snake and over it is suspended a pot from which water drips to cool the *linga*. The Mahakal *linga* is unique for two reasons, the first that it is south facing, and is therefore known as *dakshinamurti*; the second that the *linga* is supposed to have appeared on its own, *swayambhu*. The Bhashma *aarti* in the temple takes place before dawn, when the *linga* is covered with ashes.

Almost equally famous, along the river is the Kala Bhairava Temple in which liquor is offered to the gods. Another interesting shrine is the Harsiddhi Temple which is perhaps the most important *shaktipeetha* in the country. According to Hindu mythology, when Lord Shiva was carrying the burning body of his consort Sati, her elbow fell in Ujjain, consecrating the spot where the Harsiddhi Temple is located today.

A fascinating aspect of Indian civilisation is the fact of its continuity from prehistoric times to the present. Varanasi and Ujjain are examples of cities that have survived for centuries. In the best traditions of continuity, institutions in Ujjain connect with its classical traditions. The Vikram Kirti Mandir houses the Scindia Oriental Research Institute, an art gallery, a museum and an auditorium. The institute not only has a rare collection of 18,000 manuscripts on various subjects, but a reference library for oriental scholars is also present in the campus.

Similarly, the Kalidasa Academy, set up by the Government of Madhya Pradesh, is a multidisciplinary institution to project the genius of the entire classical tradition, whose foremost figure is Kalidasa. Its facilities consist of lecture halls, a theatre and a museum. The academy also provides facilities for budding scholars to undertake research work in Sanskrit, classical and traditional performing arts.

Ujjain with its many faceted attractions is a memorable experience for almost all who visit the city, despite the fact that they may have dissimilar interests and backgrounds. A trip to Ujjain connects one with much of the core of what is truly Indian.

RIGHT

A sadhu at Mahakaleshwara Temple, Ujjain.

So ends this narrative. I hope that the accounts do tempt visitors not only to explore the myriad places of interest and attractions that Madhya Pradesh has to offer, but also to read more about these as well as meet its unusual people. I have greatly enjoyed writing the text because it describes a part of India that has both captivated and mesmerised me.

And what is it that is so special about Madhya Pradesh? Madhya Pradesh is special because it has over a thousand monuments, representing lakhs of years of civilisation, in a remarkably fine state of preservation; because it has the finest forests and wild life sanctuaries of the country; because it has retreats totally unspoilt; because it has Mandu, which is not a monument but an entire medieval city built for joy; because it has the Narmada, that cascades, flows and blesses; because it has a people who are naturally gentle, tolerant and welcoming to all from other parts of the country; and finally, because it remains the very heart of India.

LEFT

Rupmati's Pavilion, Mandu.

PAGES 88 – 89

A panoramic view of the majestic Jahaz Mahal, Mandu.

The heart of Incredible India

HOTEL LISTINGS

Madhya Pradesh State Tourism Development Corporation Ltd.
For online bookings and latest tariff, please visit us at *www.mptourism.com*

Tariff as on 15.10.2009
Tariff subject to change without prior notice
Taxes extra as applicable
AP: American Plan, CP: Continental Plan
Facilities

Restaurant · Bar · Transport · Conference · Swimming pool

S. No.	Unit	Category	No. of rooms	Tariff (Rs.) Single	Double	Extra Person	Facilities
	AMARKANTAK						
1	Holiday Homes Tel: (07629) 269416 E-mail: hhamarkantak@mptourism.com	AC Aircooled AC Tent Family Room	6 4 10 2	1190 690 990 790	1190 690 990 790	300 200 250 -	Restaurant, Conference
	BANDHAVGARH						
2	White Tiger Forest Lodge Telefax: (07627) 265406, 265366 E-mail: wtfl@mptourism.com	AC Aircooled	26 12	3290 2290	3890 2890 *(AP rates - inclusive of taxes)*	800 700	Restaurant, Bar, Transport, Conference, Swimming pool
	BARGI						
3	Maikal Resort (CP) Tel: (0761) 2914577, 09425324211 E-mail: mrbargi@mptourism.com	AC	6	1590	1590	250	Restaurant
	BHEDAGHAT						
4	Motel Marble Rocks (CP) Tel: (0761) 2830424 E-mail: mmr@mptourism.com	AC Aircooled	6 5	1190 990	1190 990	175 150	Restaurant, Conference

S. No.	Unit	Category	No. of rooms	Tariff (Rs.) Single	Double	Extra Person	Facilities
	BHIMBETKA						
5	Highway Treat Tel : (07480) 281558 E-mail: bhimbetka@mptourism.com	AC	3	890	890	150	
	BHOPAL						
6	Palash Residency *** (CP) Tel: (0755) 2553006 2553066, 2553076, 3259000 Telefax: (0755) 2577441 E-mail: palash@mptourism.com	AC Suite AC Dlx AC	6 2 29	4990 2790 2290	4990 2990 2490	500 500 500	
	अशोक ग्रुप The Ashok Group						
7	Hotel Lake View Ashok*** Tel: (0755) 2660090-93 E-mail: hlvashok@sancharnet.in	Standard AC Suite AC	39 4	4500 7000	4500 7000	750 750	
	BIAORA						
8	Tourist Motel (CP) Tel : (07374) 234333 E-mail: biaora@mptourism.com	AC	6	990	990	250	
	CHANDERI						
9	Tana Bana (CP) Tel: (07547) 252222 E-mail: chanderi@mptourism.com	AC Dlx AC Aircooled	1 4 5	990 890 590	990 890 590	150 150 100	
	CHITRAKOOT						
10	Tourist Bungalow Tel: (07670) 265326 E-mail: chitrakoot@mptourism.com	AC Aircooled Dormitory beds	8 9 12	1090 690 125	1090 690 -	150 100 -	
	DATIA						
11	Tourist Motel (CP) Tel: (07522) 238125 E-mail: datia@mptourism.com	AC	4	890	890	150	
	DELAWADI						
12	Jungle Camp Mob. 09300548401 Email: delawadi@mptourism.com	AC Tent (4 Bedded) Tent	7 1	2190 2990 *(AP rates - inclusive of taxes)*	2690 -	700 -	

S. No.	Unit	Category	No. of rooms	Tariff (Rs.) Single	Double	Extra Person	Facilities
	GWALIOR						
13	Tansen Residency*** (CP) Tel: (0751) 2340370 3249000, 4010555,4010666 E-mail: tansen@mptourism.com	AC Dlx Suite AC	12 24	3290 1690	3290 1690	500 300	
	HALALI						
14	Halali Retreat Tel: 0932192848 E-mail: halali@mptourism.com	AC	2	1690	2190	600	
				(AP rates - inclusive of taxes)			
	JABALPUR						
15	Kalchuri Residency*** (CP) Tel: (0761) 2678491/92, 3269000 Telefax: (0761) 2678493 E-mail: kalchuri@mptourism.com	AC	30	1590	1590	300	
	JHABUA						
16	Tourist Motel Tel: (07392) 244668 E-mail: jhabua@mptourism.com	AC	10	990	990	150	
	KANHA						
17	Baghira Log Huts, Kisli Telefax: (07649) 277227, 277211 E-mail: blh@mptourism.com	AC Dlx AC	4 12	3990 3290	4590 3890	890 790	
				(AP rates - inclusive of taxes)			
18	Tourist Hostel, Kisli Tel: (07649) 277310 E-mail: thk@mptourism.com	Dormitory Beds	24	690	-	-	
				(AP rates - inclusive of taxes)			
19	Kanha Safari Lodge, Mukki Tel: (07636) 290715, (07637) 296029 E-mail: ksl@mptourism.com	AC Aircooled	6 6	2590 1890	3190 2490	700 700	
				(AP rates - inclusive of taxes)			
	KATNI						
20	Tourist Motel (CP) Tel: (07622) 262281-82 E-mail: katni@mptourism.com	AC Aircooled	10 4	990 790	1190 990	200 150	

S. No.	Unit	Category	No. of rooms	Tariff (Rs.) Single	Double	Extra Person	Facilities
	KHAJURAHO						
21	Hotel Jhankar (CP) Tel: (07686) 274063, 274194 E-mail: jhankar@mptourism.com	AC	19	1490	1490	200	
22	Hotel Payal (CP) Tel: (07686) 274064, 274076 E-mail: payal@mptourism.com	AC Aircooled	14 11	1490 890	1490 890	200 100	
23	Tourist Village (CP) Tel: (07686) 274062 E-mail: tvkhj@mptourism.com	AC	9	1490	1490	200	
	KHALGHAT						
24	Tourist Motel Tel: (07291) 263564, 263743 E-mail: khalghat@mptourism.com	AC AC Dlx	6 4	990 1190	990 1190	200 300	
	MADLA (PANNA)						
25	Jungle Camp Tel: 09827749975 E-mail: jcmadla@mptourism.com	AC Tent	9	2590 *(AP rates - inclusive of taxes)*	2890	790	
	MAHESHWAR						
26	Narmada Retreat (CP) Tel: (07283) 273455 E-mail: maheshwar@mptourism.com	AC Dlx/Tent AC/Tent Aircooled *(4 bedded family room)*	10 10 3	1590 1290 1290 *(No CP rates on 4 bedded family room)*	1590 1290 -	200 200 -	
	MAIHAR						
27	Hotel Surbahar Tel: (07674) 233362 E-mail:maihar@mptourism.com	AC Dlx AC Aircooled Dormitory Beds	1 5 5 26	1290 890 590 125	1290 890 590 -	200 150 100 -	
	MANDLA						
28	Tourist Motel (CP) Tel: (07642) 260599 E-mail: mandla@mptourism.com	AC Aircooled	4 8	1090 890	1090 890	200 150	
	MANDU						
29	Malwa Resort (CP) Tel: (07292) 263235	AC Aircooled	10 10	1890 1190	1890 1190	200 150	

S. No.	Unit	Category	No. of rooms	Tariff(Rs.) Single	Double	Extra Person	Facilities
30	Malwa Retreat (CP) Tel: (07292) 263221 E-mail: mretreatm@mptourism.com	AC Aircooled	2 6	1490 890	1490 890	200 100	
	NEEMUCH						
31	Tourist Motel Tel: (07423) 280080 Email: neemuch@mptourism.com	AC	6	890	890	150	
	OMKARESHWAR						
32	Narmada Resort (CP) Tel: (07280) 271455 E-mail: omkareshwar@mptourism.com	AC Dlx AC Aircooled (budget)	3 8 8	1590 1190 790	1590 1190 790	250 200 100	
	NOWGAON						
33	Highway Treat (CP) Tel: (07685) 256425 E-mail: nowgaon@mptourism.com	Aircooled	2	890	890	150	
	ORCHHA						
34	Betwa Retreat ***(CP) Tel: (07680) 252618, 252402 E-mail: betwa@mptourism.com	Heritage suite (AC) AC AC Tent	1 14 10	4990 1690 1290	4990 1690 1290	700 300 200	
35	Sheesh Mahal (Heritage Hotel)(CP) Telefax: (07680) 252624 E-mail: smorchha@mptourism.com	Maharaja Suite (AC) Maharani Suite (AC) AC AC Single	1 1 5 1	4990 3990 1690 1190	4990 3990 1690 -	700 300 200 -	
	PACHMARHI						
36	Amaltas Tel: (07578) 252098 E-mail: amaltas@mptourism.com	AC Dlx AC	5 5	1890 1590	1890 1590	250 200	
37	Champak Bungalow Tel: (07578) 285315, 285316 E-mail: champak@mptourism.com	AC Dlx AC Tent AC	7 5 7	4190 2790 2790 *(AP rates - inclusive of taxes)*	4690 3290 3290	1090 990 990	
38	Glen View Tel: (07578) 252533, 252445 E-mail: gview@mptourism.com	AC Dlx AC AC Tent	6 15 4	4190 2790 2790 *(AP rates - inclusive of taxes)*	4690 3290 3290	1090 990 990	

S. No.	Unit	Category	No. of rooms	Tariff (Rs.)			Facilities
				Single	Double	Extra Person	
39	Hilltop Bungalow Tel: (07578) 252846 E-mail: hilltop@mptourism.com	AC	5	1890	1890	250	
40	Hotel Highlands Tel: (07578) 252099,252399 E-mail: highland@mptourism.com	AC Aircooled	20 20	1490 990	1490 990	200 200	
41	Panchvati Tel: (07578) 252096 E-mail: panchvati@mptourism.com	Aircooled (cottages) AC (huts)	5 5	1690 1890	1690 1890	250 250	
42	Rock-End Manor Tel: (07578) 252079 E-mail: rem@mptourism.com	AC Dlx	6	4190 *(AP rates - inclusive of taxes)*	4690	1090	
43	Satpura Retreat Tel: (07578) 252097 E-mail: satpura@mptourism.com	AC Dlx AC Standard	2 4	4190 3590 *(AP rates - inclusive of taxes)*	4690 4290	1090 890	
44	Woodland Bungalow (DIB) Tel : (07578) 252272 E-mail: woodlands@mptourism.com	Aircooled	4	990	990	200	
	PENCH						
45	Kipling's Court Tel: (07695) 232830,232850 E-mail: kcpench@mptourism.com	AC Aircooled Dormitory Beds	15 5 10	3240 2290 700 *(AP rates - inclusive of taxes)*	3890 2890 -	800 690 -	
	PIPARIYA						
46	Tourist Motel Tel: (07576) 222299 E-mail: pipariya@mptourism.com	AC	4	890	890	200	
	ROOKHAD						
47	Highway Treat Tel: (07695) 290130 E-mail: rookhad@mptourism.com	Aircooled	4	490	490	100